The Mathematics of Bookselling

A Monograph

The Mathematics of Bookselling

A Monograph

LEONARD SHATZKIN
Author of "In Cold Type"

Sun River Press

Published by Sun River Press
ISBN 0-87838-025-6

Text and Cover design and execution by Celie Fitzgerald

To order copies of this book:
Cost is $10.00 per copy plus $3.00 Shipping and Handling per order. Pennsylvania residents, add 6% State Sales Tax; New York residents, add applicable State Sales Tax.

Visa and MasterCard accepted. Include Account Number and Expiration Date.

Checks should be made payable to The Butterick Company.

Send order (prepaid only) to:
The Butterick Company Inc.
PO Box 1752
Altoona, PA 16603

THE MATHEMATICS OF BOOKSELLING

A Monograph

Foreword

Book retailing seems fairly straightforward, requiring no more than addition and subtraction to explain or control it. The bookseller converts money into books, and then converts the books back into money — enough "more money" than the books originally cost to cover the expenses of the entire operation and a little extra.

It is *not* that simple.

The most serious obstacle to sound bookselling practice is rarely examined, or even acknowledged. It is the way in which the bookseller keeps track of the operation of the business and the mistaken business strategy that results.

Conventional bookstore accounting, almost universally applied among booksellers, measures the store's financial performance against sales. The key component in that measurement is perceived to be the difference between what the books cost the bookseller and what the bookseller sells them for — the gross profit or gross margin. When books are sold at retail, the gross margin is equal to the discount at which the bookseller purchased them. From the gross margin, the expenses of operating the store are subtracted to arrive at the net profit or loss.

Unfortunately, that gross margin return on sales, the GMROS, tells us nothing about how well the bookseller has invested money, step one in the conversion and re-conversion process. Two booksellers, each with one million dollars in sales, may show a gross margin on sales of $400,000 (an average discount of 40 percent delivered) or 40 percent of sales. They accept the idea that they have equivalent financial results, even though one has an average investment in book inventory of $150,000 (a gross margin of $2.67 per dollar of investment) while the other has an investment of $600,000 (a gross margin of 67¢ per dollar of investment). The first bookseller is investing more wisely and is much more likely to get rich faster — but, using the GMROS measure, the accountant's numbers give no hint of that whatever.

If the bookseller were buying a book*store* instead of *books*, return on the *investment* required to buy the store would be much more the issue than return on *sales*. And, of course, it should be after the bookseller owns the store.

A much more useful number than the GMROS — certainly more helpful for guiding the conversion of money into books — is the gross margin return on inventory investment (GMROII), which measures how productively the bookseller uses working capital. The gross margin return on inventory investment is calculated as the product of the margin (the difference between what the bookseller pays for the books and what the bookseller gets for them) multiplied by the number of times each invested dollar has been sold and reinvested that year — which we call stock turn.

Unfortunately, most booksellers do not calculate stock turn, and even fewer measure its effect on their financial performance.

Stock turn is easy enough to ignore because nothing in the daily operation of the store *forces* it on the bookseller's attention. There are always many other matters that seem more pressing.

Complications force the bookseller to make all kinds of subsidiary decisions and to make sometimes difficult choices among alternatives. In order to convert money into books, the bookseller must choose the titles and decide the quantities. To select among titles not yet published, the bookseller usually has the assistance of the publisher's representative, who presents the bookstore buyer with information on forthcoming titles and suggests the number of each the store should have. This is helpful, but the information from some sales representatives is more consistently reliable than it is from others, and, in any case, the bookseller is aware that the representative's income depends, usually directly, on the size of the order the rep gets from the bookseller. And many publishers' reps fail to call on many stores. In fact, some smaller publishers have no reps at all.

Many of the bookseller's decisions apply not to forthcoming titles but to titles already in the store. Should additional copies be acquired of this or that title? Should the remaining copies of this or that title be returned to the publisher for credit? For such decisions, the publisher's rep is rarely helpful, or even available, in a timely fashion.

In addition to the need for knowledge of the store's clientele and of the books and their probable salability, selection of titles and quantities is further complicated by considerations of discount and the right to return and terms of return. Publishers differ in the discounts they offer for orders of different quantities and combinations of titles. Although the recent trend is toward a flatter discount, traditionally the larger the order, the higher the discount. But the larger the order, the greater the danger that copies will have to be returned (assuming, of course, that the publisher accepts overstock returns). Each publisher has different rules: the time frame in which returns will be accepted; whether full or partial credit will be given; whether prior permission is required; whether credit balances are refundable or must be used toward future purchases.

Buying additional copies (and sometimes buying the original copies) requires the bookseller to decide whether to get them directly from the publisher or from a wholesaler. The decision may be to do both: to get a few "emergency" copies from the wholesaler and the principal amount from the publisher. The wholesaler usually sells at a lower, less favorable, discount than the publisher but supplies books more quickly and allows booksellers to combine titles across publishers' lists. Wholesalers usually enforce prompt payment, whereas publishers are more inclined to accept tardy payment without penalty. The consequences of being cut off by a wholesaler can be more severe. Temporarily losing the services of a wholesaler effectively undercuts placing special orders and forces the bookseller, even for normal replenishment, to permit some titles to remain out of stock until a qualifying order for that publisher can be accumulated.

Better discounts from publishers depend on orders large enough (from each publisher) to reach an attractive "discount step," although, as mentioned previously, this number may now be relatively low. That can be a lot easier working from a large publisher's list than a small publisher's list. Rather than lose discount, the bookseller may allow some titles to be out of stock for a time while waiting for an order to reach an acceptable size. On top of any discount advantages, buying directly from the publisher — original and additional copies — is considered to be a factor in getting co-operative advertising money from the publisher, in assuring that the rep will continue to call, in participating in author tours, and in qualifying for other benefits the publisher offers.

Deciding title by title and order by order what to buy and in what combination is often strongly influenced by the very clear and obvious discount advantages associated with each decision. It seems possible to evaluate such decisions straightforwardly, using discount as a guide. But even if that guide were valid for title-by-title decisions, what guide should the bookseller use for determining how broadly the store's assortment of titles should range? Breadth of inventory is usually not consciously decided — it is what results from all the individual title-by-title decisions — to buy, to hold, or to return. What is left is the breadth of assortment.

The bookseller may have to decide whether to offer

discounts to retail customers — and on what titles and how much. The question usually arises because a competitive store, frequently a chain branch, is discounting and a negative effect on sales is evident.

It is generally accepted among booksellers that, except for the obvious discount percentages and their seemingly direct effect on the margin any book can earn when sold, there are no reliable numbers to guide their day-to-day decisions. Guidance — except for the simple aim of getting the highest discount to maximize earnings — is supposed to come from the nonquantifiable sense of "being a bookseller," who can distill experience into a knowledgeable attitude that makes it possible to judge which titles to stock, how many copies, when and how many to reorder, what and when to return. Whatever the reasons — differences in bookstore clientele, differences in bookseller personalities, the confusion of thousands of titles moving through the system — booksellers have not found a useful mathematically based navigational system for managing a bookstore, such as the sky's stars offer ships' captains.

Above all, as navigators, we need to know where we want to go. The bookseller is in the business of turning working capital into books, which are the bookseller's "inventory investment," and then books back into working capital. The objective is to make buying and stocking decisions that will produce the greatest contribution from that inventory investment.

The Mathematics of Bookselling

A Monograph

BUYING: The Bookseller's Most Critical Activity

Although buying is certainly not the only preoccupation for the bookseller nor the only one that demands investment, buying does deserve and get the most management attention and the largest portion of available working capital. Expenses other than the cost of merchandise — for example, rent, personnel, etc. — are relatively fixed, and changes up or down (such as adding or subtracting a clerk or a cash register) do not substantially affect the operating statement. The book inventory — the breadth and depth of the titles available to the public that result from the buying activity — is the most powerful lever for profitability in the bookseller's business.

Buying books is the key activity in the bookseller's "business" of turning money into books and books back into money, and it is clearly the most important. The economic health of the bookstore depends more on what titles are bought and, even more important, how they are bought than on anything else the book retailer does. Buying takes the most time of all bookstore activities, and it is the task assigned to the most capable people available.

Conceptually, buying must be approached on two levels. The strategic level consists of setting out the broad objectives that the selection and breadth of titles in the store is intended to achieve: the audience that the bookseller wishes to attract and serve, the overall level of investment in books to be maintained (probably varying with the time of year), the average targeted range of stock turn, the stance toward "special ordering" titles not in stock and the level of service to be offered for such orders, and the like. These are matters which are the province of top management or, in the case of the small store owned and operated by a single person, the bookseller wearing a top management hat. Success in achieving these strategic objectives can be, at least broadly, measured. The bookseller knows the investment in inventory, the stock turn, the activity in each subject category in the store, and the number of special orders each month and their distribution among subject categories.

The tactical buying level consists of the day-by-day, title-by-title decisions necessary to bring the store as close as possible to the strategic objectives. The bookseller cannot usually deal with these decisions in as deliberate and relaxed a manner as when dealing with strategy. Tactical decisions are presented to the bookseller, title by title, when a publisher's rep calls and presents a forthcoming list; when a book is sold and (particularly if that is the last copy) replenishment must be considered; when someone reviews the special orders and finds a title occurring more than once. The decision on each title is made at that point: whether to order it or reorder it and, if yes, how many copies. The decision may be not to buy or not to reorder. Negative decisions may result in fewer returns but may be more costly to the store in lost sales in the long run.

In recognition of its importance, bookstore management usually retains control over every buying decision. In the case of large stores or bookstore chains, where the number of decisions precludes tight central supervision, the responsibility is delegated down to lower-level managers, each of whom presumably has some special expertise, usually knowledge of the subject category, to help buy profitably.

Buying is handicapped by the assignment of important people to do it, expecting them to ponder carefully over each decision — instead of finding a way to make buying decisions more routinely by the application of tested rules.

Assigning the task to management puts an uncalculated but, nevertheless, very real minimum on the size of any order that can be economically considered. The decision must be worth management's time. It is not very sensible to spend five dollars of time puzzling over whether to buy one copy of a ten-dollar paperback. And it argues for fewer orders more carefully arrived at. Buying the same total number of copies of a title in a series of cautious orders costs more in management time than getting all the copies needed in one order placed at the very beginning. Even with delegation of responsibility, there is only so much buying time available. This creates a bottleneck that limits the number of titles a store of a given sales volume can permit, and depresses the stock turn a store with a given number of titles can achieve.

Although booksellers do not currently divide them that way, it is useful to distinguish between two types of buying decisions. The first — a prepublication order being the best example — are those for which no objective data are available to guide the decisions. There may be analogous information (for example, the sale of a supposedly comparable title, the visibility of the author or the subject, the size of the announced promotion budget), but there is no direct sales experience with that title.

The second type of buying decision — the reorder of a staple backlist title being the purest example — are those for which some direct sales experience exists to provide objective hints of how well additional copies of that title will sell.

The first type of decision (buying situations for which no pertinent sales data are available) can only be made by management, applying its best judgment to whatever indirect evidence it wishes to consider.

For the second type of decision (limited to reordering of

titles previously placed into inventory by buying management), subjective management judgment is not necessarily superior to the application of objective rules derived from actual sales experience. Also, this category may include decisions for which the cost of management's time cancels any advantage the decision, positive or negative, might offer. For example: A ten-dollar book has been sold that has been in inventory for three months (four times turn, not bad); should it be reordered or do the odds suggest that it be dropped? What are the chances that a buying manager or an expert in the subject category will make the right decision and do it fast enough to do it economically?

The overwhelming percentage of titles are (or should be) in the store in single copies and should be reordered in single copies or deliberately not reordered; because the need for so many decisions is pressuring management, titles may simply be overlooked. If the one copy of *Better Chess Endgames* has been sold after three months, given the very obvious influence of pure chance in the sale of anything, can the expert on leisure pastimes, or on chess, or even on chess endgames, decide with confidence whether to replace that copy? Why should anyone believe that buying management or the category expert is competent to make that decision?

The answer is that probably no one really does. Responsibility for these decisions is handed to some level of human management because there seems to be no alternative. The decisions must be made by the bookseller to safeguard the bookseller's interest and to prevent raids on the store's working capital. They cannot be entrusted to the publisher, even though the publisher has much more data to help make the decisions, because the publisher cannot be trusted to decide objectively or in the store's interest. The bookseller's working capital is too valuable an instrument to be entrusted to any but top management or those selected by top management.

The store's buying decisions are the heart (and mind) of the bookselling business, and, we most certainly agree, not to be handled lightly. But current practice, though avoiding the cost of decisions by those who may not be sufficiently concerned with the store's well-being, incurs the cost of decisions poorly made, whether they are positive (to buy) or negative (not to buy). We consider here only the costs to the bookseller, not the costs to the publisher in returns, overprinting, unrealized sale of midlist and minor titles, sales reps to call on stores and telemarketers to follow up, etc.

The most important cost of this cumbersome process for most stores is the resulting narrowness of the title assortment and, in most cases, low stock turn, even though a narrow assortment theoretically permits a high turn at retail. What the narrow assortment costs in reduced store traffic is suggested by the sharp influx of customer traffic experienced by chain superstores when they were opened, with 100,000 or 150,000 titles in neighborhoods that already had stores with 20,000 to 50,000 titles. The pent-up demand indicates how much business the bookstores had passed up for years because buying practice offered an inadequate range of titles. Sales were lost on titles not on hand that should have been.

The book world is somewhat more familiar with the other side of the coin — the unsold books that go back as returns. In the present situation, since the new superstores are so jealously protecting their advertised 100,000-title stock levels that they have not cleared out their overstocks, we do not yet know whether the best 100,000 have been selected sensibly, and how economically that stock level can be maintained. The low stock turns, the slowing of payment to publishers to soften the effect of poor stock turn on cash flow, and the growing accounts payable showing on chains' annual statements strongly suggest that, at some point soon (this is written in February 1997), an avalanche of buying mistakes will move from chain superstores to publishers' warehouses.

There are other costs, including the cost of the time invested in making all those decisions. In the case of sole proprietorships and small bookstores, it is time that would be more profitably invested in bookselling activities; in the case of chains, it is a cost represented by a small army of "buyers."

DISCOUNT VERSUS STOCK TURN: A First Overview

Discount and stock turn are key numbers in the economics — and the mathematics — of bookselling. Discount is the difference between the retail price of the book and its cost to the bookseller. If the bookseller sells at full retail, the discount is the gross margin earned, but even if the book is discounted to the consumer, the higher the discount earned from the vendor, the greater the gross margin.

Stock turn is the number of times each dollar invested in book inventory is sold and reinvested in one year. It is not so clearly obvious as discount; it cannot be known in advance as discount can. Stock turn must be calculated, only after the books have been on sale for some months, by dividing total sales by average inventory, both figures at retail price or both at cost.

Discount and stock turn are not usually considered to be in opposition to each other, probably because stock turn gets very little detailed study. We consider one "versus" the other for two reasons. First, either discount or stock turn can serve as a simple benchmark to guide buying for the bookstore. In addition, under the traditional publisher discount schedules, a larger order earns a larger discount but a larger order takes longer to sell, so a larger order "earns" a lower stock turn.

As our calculations (below) demonstrate conclusively, because each additional point of discount adds slightly more than four percent to the margin earned per dollar invested, it is self-defeating for the bookseller to increase the order by more than four percent to gain a point of discount.

The best way to consider which compass might best serve to steer buying decisions is to coldly evaluate the one numerical guide currently so dear to booksellers: the discount. Discount is assumed to be the straightforward, logical, incontrovertible indicator of how much margin the book will contribute when it is sold. Unfortunately, discount, in bookstore navigation, is analogous to what the "earth is flat" doctrine was to terrestrial navigation — so obvious that it is taken to be self-evident, yet, on critical examination, found to be completely misleading.

Let's start by examining the most fundamental mathematical truth in book retailing. The gross profit (margin) earned by each dollar of working capital invested in book inventory is produced by a combination of two factors: the discount, which determines how much each invested dollar earns when it is sold; and the stock turn, the speed at which the invested dollar is sold and reinvested. The margin per dollar (discount divided by cost) multiplied by the stock turn is the gross margin earned per invested dollar.

Discount and cost are known in advance. Discount is right there in the publisher's terms of sale and on the publisher's invoice. Each copy of each book has a cost precisely knowable in advance. The step in discount is frequently the reason the order placed by the bookseller was for x plus one copy rather than x copies. Stock turn, however, *cannot* be known in advance, simply because stock turn does not exist in advance. Stock turn must be calculated, after the books are sold, by dividing total sales by the average inventory. At the time stock turn can be known — after all the copies of all the titles on an order have been sold or returned — it is too late for it to influence the buying decision. Booksellers rarely bother to calculate stock turn, and we never met one who calculated it title by title or by the books on any one order.

Stock turn can be calculated by dividing the annual sales by the average value of the inventory. If sales are tallied at retail price, the value of the inventory (the average of the inventory on hand) must also be at retail price. If sales are tallied at (or can be converted to) value at cost, the inventory should be valued at cost. Or, stock turn for a title can be measured by dividing the number of copies sold by the average number of copies in inventory. Stock turn on total inventory can be calculated against the annual sales for the entire store, or on some subject category (children's books, for example) comparing inventory against the corresponding sales (of children's books). It can also be calculated by publisher (as we shall see that Under Cover Books did) or by titles bought from wholesalers rather than direct (as we shall see that Harry W. Schwartz Bookshops did), or by season of the year, or by price point, or by whatever division seems worth examining — but stock turn must be *calculated;* it is not self-evident.

Stock turn is the measure of how long books sit in the store before they are sold to give back the dollars to invest in other books. It is a measure of the *productivity* of working capital. It is a measure of how much sales a dollar of inventory will produce in any unit of time.

Working capital — in the form of *books* — which is sitting around not getting changed back into working capital in the form of *cash for buying more books* is not being productive.

Return on sales — the currently accepted measure of bookselling success — depends on the difference between what you get for the book and what it cost you. If the book is sold at the retail price, that difference is the discount. All other things being equal, the higher the discount, the higher the margin, and, therefore, the higher the percentage return on sales. Fixation on return on sales makes it natural that the bookseller should seem to be fixated on discount.

Average discount is all you need to know (in addition to sales) to calculate the gross margin return on sales (GMROS). To calculate the gross margin return on inventory investment (GMROII), in addition to discount, you need to know — or, rather, to calculate — the stock turn.

Failure to give proper weight to stock turn inclines the bookseller to exaggerate the importance of discount. Although the situation is changing rapidly as more and more publishers offer a higher flat discount regardless of the size of the order, the traditional pattern of publishers' discounts has been that the discount goes up as the size of the order goes up.

Why do publishers offer higher discounts?

It is an inducement to the bookseller to increase the order — and there is no question that, more often than not, it works! Quantity discount is supposed to be a kind of reward which will make the bookseller happier, and a little bit richer. It is sincerely offered, and it costs the publisher a lot of out-of-pocket money. How much good does it do the bookseller?

On a one thousand dollar order, the difference between 40 percent discount and 45 percent discount is fifty dollars. That fifty dollars comes right out of the publisher's pocket, and the publisher is sure it is going right into the bookseller's pocket. The notion that a higher discount may be costly both to the publisher and the bookseller seems too crazy to be taken seriously. But we shall see that it is often costly to the bookseller.

As we have said, the bookseller's annual income per dollar of investment in books equals the margin each dollar earns (discount divided by cost) multiplied by the stock turn, which depends directly on how long it takes to sell the books the bookseller buys. How long it will take to sell any copy cannot be predicted, but it is conservative to assume that if an order for books is increased by 10 percent, it will take 10 percent longer to sell the books in that order.

If, on a larger order, the increase in discount results in an increase in margin of 10 percent and it takes less than 10 percent longer to sell the books in the larger order, the bookseller will be richer; if it takes exactly 10 percent longer to sell the books, the bookseller will be even; if it takes more than 10 percent longer to sell the books, the bookseller would be better off with the original order.

The table below shows the bookseller's margin per dollar at each step in discount between 40 percent and 50 percent and how much the margin goes up at each discount step. Therefore, it demonstrates how much an order can be increased to get higher discount before the

Relating Margin Earned to Order Size at Each Discount Step

Discount Step	*Margin Earned per Dollar*	*Increase in Margin Over Lower Discount Step*	*% Increase in Margin Over Lower Discount Step*	*% Increase in Order Over Which One Discount Point Reduces Income*
40%	.40 ÷ .60 = .6667			
41%	.41 ÷ .59 = .6949	.0282	4.23	4.23%
42%	.42 ÷ .58 = .7241	.0292	4.20	4.20%
43%	.43 ÷ .57 = .7544	.0303	4.18	4.18%
44%	.44 ÷ .56 = .7857	.0313	4.15	4.15%
45%	.45 ÷ .55 = .8182	.0325	4.14	4.14%
46%	.46 ÷ .54 = .8519	.0337	4.12	4.12%
47%	.47 ÷ .53 = .8868	.0349	4.10	4.10%
48%	.48 ÷ .52 = .9231	.0363	4.09	4.09%
49%	.49 ÷ .51 = .9608	.0377	4.08	4.08%
50%	.50 ÷ .50 = 1.0000	.0392	4.08	4.08%

bookseller's income per dollar goes down instead of up.

As the table clearly shows, each point of discount adds only four and a small fraction percent to the margin per dollar invested. The additional margin for the discount step between 40 percent and 41 percent is almost the same as between 49 percent and 50 percent. Therefore, any increase in the size of the order greater than four and a small fraction percent wipes out the advantage of one point of discount; an eight and a fraction percent increase in the size of the order wipes out the advantage of two percentage points of additional discount.

For instance, on an order for 100 assorted copies that earns 41 percent, if the discount step to 42 percent involves buying more than 104 copies (100 x 1.042 percent), don't reach for it.

Or, looked at another way, if the order is intended to cover needs for about one month, one discount point extends the selling time by 1.2 days before gross profit (the product of margin and stock turn) starts to decline. (All this may become an interesting historical footnote as the movement by publishers away from discount steps becomes more widespread.)

The recent growing shift in publishers' discount schedules from steps based on quantity to the "flat discount" offering 45 percent or more on any order above a small minimum eliminates the strongest argument publishers had to influence booksellers to ratchet up advance orders. That is certainly not the publishers' intention, and it will probably take a while for this change in discount practice to result in the logical reduction in the size of advance orders, but it is likely to come.

There have been two pressing reasons for the long-overdue change in discount practice. For many years — until very recently — the Federal Trade Commission, in a kind of relaxed bureaucratic way, had been arguing that publishers' discount steps could not legally exceed the actual saving to the publisher in filling the larger order. Even more serious, the FTC held that the most a publisher saved, from the smallest order to the largest, was two percent, so the total range of discount steps for quantity should be held to two points rather than the six or eight points found in many discount schedules.

Though the arguments were not the same as those advanced by the American Booksellers Association in its lawsuits against publishers — initiated when it became clear that the FTC had the patience to delay enforcement until independent bookstores disappeared — enforcement might have precluded the need for the lawsuits. Fortunately, the ABA lawsuits were successful in obtaining consent decrees resulting in higher discounts on smaller quantities, because the FTC abruptly dropped its inquiry and simply walked away from the problem.

The flat discount blunts any argument that publishers are favoring large customers over small ones.

Another reason for offering an attractive flat discount is the publishers' growing realization of how much more business from bookstores is moving through wholesalers, costing publishers the difference between the retailer discount and the wholesaler discount. The bookseller's reliance on the wholesaler reduces the occasions for the publisher to be in contact with the bookseller to influence the nature of the reorder. The publishers' attractive flat discount, given the booksellers' overfixation on discount as the key to their success, is likely to attract some of that business back to the publisher.

THE UNDER COVER BOOKS EXPERIENCE: Discount Versus Stock Turn

As an unexpected by-product of an experiment with buying strategy, the Turners, owners of Under Cover Books, accumulated detailed information that would otherwise be

very difficult to collect. Analysis of that unusual trove of detail revealed that the correlation between stock turn and profit is absolute and unmistakable. The correlation between discount and profit, on the other hand, though it must certainly exist, is so tenuous that it cannot be discerned in one year's experience with books from 165 publishers.

The relationship between discount and stock turn — the contribution of each factor toward generating bookstore profit — was demonstrated dramatically in the data carefully compiled by Under Cover Books (now Under Cover Book Service). Over a period of many months in 1982 and 1983, the Turners kept careful records, by publisher by month, of all orders placed, books received, discounts and net costs, sales, inventory level, and just about every detail connected with the purchases, sales, and inventory of every publisher with whom Under Cover had dealings.

The Turners were kind enough to give me the figures for one year, 1982, and we tried to find some meaning in the data.

The most significant and startling fact to come out of that study was a dramatic confirmation of the relationship we have just examined: the difference between the effect of discount and the effect of stock turn on income from sales.

We compared the average (delivered) discount on books bought from each of the 165 publishers on whom Under Cover kept records that year with the income (the gross margin per invested dollar) from that publisher's books. Since discount seemed so important, one expected that the higher the discount from any publisher, the higher would be the gross margin from that publisher's books.

We made a similar comparison of stock turn against gross margin from each publisher's books.

To make the tabulations easier to understand, the numbers were put into graphs.

Rather than bore you with the actual tabulations, publisher by publisher, of discount against gross margin (margin per dollar multiplied by stock turn) and stock turn against gross margin, we present you with the graphs of each tabulation from the Under Cover Books experience.

Let us look at the first graph (Figure A), showing discount against gross margin return on inventory investment.

The discount is shown horizontally, increasing from left to right. The gross margin return per dollar invested is shown vertically, increasing with increasing height. The publisher whose books were bought at an average discount (delivered) of, say, 41 percent and resulted in earning a gross margin of $3.00 per dollar invested would be represented by a small "x" where the line of 41 percent discount and the line of $3.00 of gross margin intersect. There are 165 such little x's on the graph.

The average discount granted by the 165 publishers varied from a low of 34 percent to a high of 47 percent — a fairly wide spread. At 34 percent discount, the bookseller earns only 51.5¢ per dollar of inventory sold; at 47 percent discount, the bookseller earns 88.7¢. Each dollar's worth of the books sold of the publisher granting the highest discount is earning 72 percent more than the dollar's worth of books of the stingiest publisher. That certainly demonstrates the power of discount!

The range of gross margin return on inventory investment among the 165 publishers was surprisingly wide — from a little over zero to almost five dollars per dollar of investment — which should indicate to booksellers how much rides on their buying decisions.

We might expect a pattern to emerge showing more x's high on the right-hand side of the graph (high gross margin), reflecting a higher average discount, and fewer

Figure A

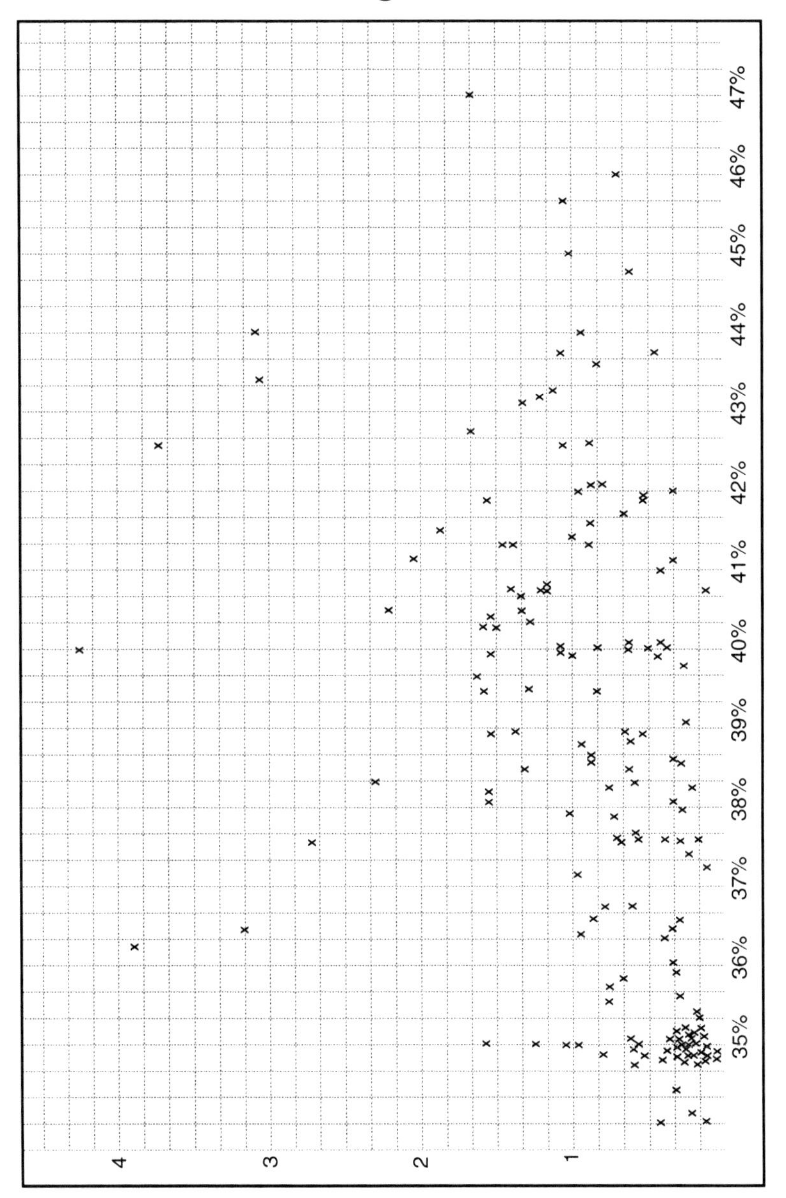
47%
46%
45%
44%
43%
42%
41%
40%
39%
38%
37%
36%
35%
4
3
2
1
Discount
Gross Margin per Dollar Invested

x's high on the graph (high gross margin) toward the left, where discount is lower. With some astigmatism and a little prejudice, perhaps you can see that.

Without astigmatism, the graph shows almost no relation — in the range of discounts from 34 percent to 47 percent — between discount and gross margin. *Consider that the second highest gross margin among all the publishers was achieved at a discount of 36.6 percent.* A publisher offering a discount most booksellers would consider to be almost unacceptably low (and is in the low range at Under Cover Books) contributed a higher gross margin than 99 percent of all the other publishers. Those data make it clear that buying at 45 percent may not necessarily make more money for the bookseller than buying at 40 percent, or even — horrors — at 36.6 percent.

The graph does not *prove* that discount and gross margin are not related — logic tells us that clearly they are. What it does show is that the relationship is so tenuous that 165 cases are not a sufficient number to reveal a pattern. In fact, this graph very strongly resembles graphs used in textbooks on differential calculus to illustrate that two variables — like flat feet and cancer of the lung — have no relationship whatever with one another.

Now let's look at Figure B, showing the relation between stock turn and gross margin.

The grid is similar, with stock turn ranging horizontally between zero and seven, and exactly the same vertical range of gross margin, from zero to five dollars. Again there are 165 x's on the graph.

Now we do have a pattern!

The lower the stock turn (left side of graph), the lower the gross margin; the higher the turn, the higher the gross margin. The pattern is so pronounced that it is possible to calculate what mathematicians call a "regression line" or "least squares line" that describes the mathematical relation

Figure B

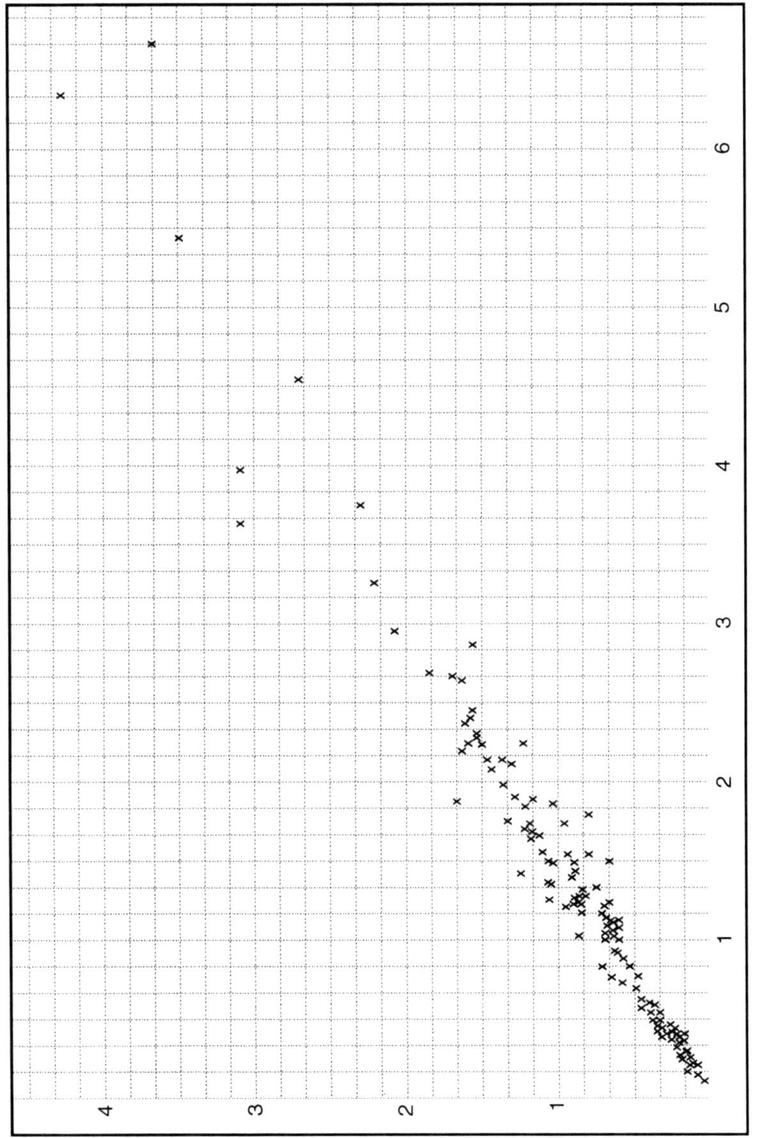

between stock turn and gross margin for Under Cover's business with these 165 publishers.

The equation for that line in this case is: $y = .663x - .012$ (in words, gross margin equals stock turn multiplied by .663, minus .012).

Since the points are tightly grouped around the "regression line," we can safely say that under the conditions at Under Cover Books, each additional turn of the stock will increase gross margin approximately 65¢ per dollar invested in inventory. The reverse is also true. For each reduction of one full turn, gross margin will decrease approximately 65¢ per dollar invested.

Comparing figures for individual publishers shows some very interesting and thought-provoking results, further underlining the importance of stock turn.

For example, Harvard and Yale, both university presses, had approximately the same level of inventory in the store. In 1982, Harvard was not generous with discount — it averaged only 38.6 percent at Under Cover. Yale was more openhanded — 43.75 percent. That generosity may have cost Yale University Press a lot of money, but it was of very little benefit to Under Cover Books. The return per dollar invested in inventory was almost twice as great from Harvard titles (in spite of lower discount) as from Yale titles. Why? Because the stock turn for Harvard titles was approximately double that of Yale's. Harvard made more money for Harvard (because of the lower average discount) and more money for Under Cover Books (despite the lower average discount). The higher discount earned Yale less money, and, paradoxically, less money for Under Cover Books as well.

A comparison of two large commercial publishers points out a similar lesson. The discount on Random House books averaged more than 43 percent compared to Simon & Schuster's average of only slightly over 40 percent. Yet

Under Cover Books earned 20 percent more gross margin per dollar invested with S&S than with Random House. Why? Because S&S stock turned one-third faster than Random House inventory.

The comparison of Yale with Harvard, or Random House with S&S, may suggest that one publisher's books produce a higher margin because that publisher's titles are better than the other's. Not at all. The literary quality or selling potential of the books has nothing to do with stock turn or the effect of stock turn on gross margin. It is all in the way the books are bought, not in which titles they are. The differences among publishers at Under Cover were accidental because the way in which the books were bought was largely accidental.

As a matter of fact, it is happenstance that caused Under Cover to provide figures separated by publisher. Because Under Cover Books was using this data to allow reps to control their own inventories, the information was gathered by publisher. If some other purpose had driven the collection of data, it might have been grouped differently. We now know that the same conclusions could have been drawn from figures comparing books from different display shelves or display tables. Any grouping of titles that provides average discount and stock turn for each group will result in comparative tabulations very similar to the ones in our two graphs. They will differ in some details, but not in the inescapable conclusion that discount has almost nothing to do with gross margin and stock turn has almost everything to do with gross margin.

The dramatic proof that how much a bookseller earns per invested dollar is much less important than how many times a year the bookseller earns it is startling. According to the notions enshrined by the accounting procedures, a bookstore's success — its profitability — is measured, after deducting cost of goods and operating expenses, by the net margin against sales. The amount of working capital immobilized by the investment in books (or everything else) plays no part in that calculation.

Even today, most booksellers seem to accept that. That is how the ABA reports bookstore profitability; it is in their *Manual on Bookselling;* it is in the *ABACUS Expanded* financial survey. It is also how booksellers report to the IRS. Without suggesting that you change your reporting to the IRS — they might not like it — we would suggest you reconsider whether those IRS numbers are the ones you should use to guide your business decisions.

A Mathematical Footnote: We are saying that between the two factors that determine the bookseller's margin — discount and stock turn — stock turn is, by far, the more important and that the bookseller is mistaken to base buying and inventory control on an overvaluation of the discount factor.

However, since this monograph is entitled "The Mathematics of Bookselling," we must admit that *mathematically, discount is the more important.* It is only the realities of retailing life that frustrate the mathematics, assigning discount the minor place.

Let me explain.

As we have already pointed out, the total gross margin (GM) the bookseller earns is the margin earned per dollar of inventory multiplied by the number of times that dollar of inventory is reinvested and sold.

The margin per dollar of inventory is the discount divided by the cost, which is simply discount divided by one minus the discount. The number of times each dollar of inventory is sold is one divided by the length of time the dollar has been sitting in inventory waiting for that happy moment or, simply, the stock turn.

Mathematically, this can be expressed by:

$$GM = \left(\frac{\text{discount}}{1 - \text{discount}}\right) (\text{stock turn})$$

Let's suppose that you manage to increase the stock turn by 10 percent, going, for example, from a turn of 3 to a turn of 3.3. It is clear that the gross margin will increase by 10 percent. Very gratifying.

Suppose that you increase the discount by 10 percent, going, for example, from a discount of 40 percent to a discount of 44 percent. At a 40 percent discount, the effect of the discount factor is .40 divided by .60 (1 minus .40), which equals .6666.

At a 44 percent discount, the effect of the discount factor is .44 divided by .56 (1 minus .44), which equals .7857.

A little calculation will show that .7857 is about 18 percent higher than .6666.

So, while a 10 percent increase in stock turn increases gross margin by 10 *percent,* a 10 percent increase in discount increases gross margin by 18 *percent* — almost double the effect. Very clearly, mathematically, a change in discount, up or down, results in a much larger change in gross margin than an equivalent change, up or down, in stock turn.

Any mathematician would thoroughly sympathize with the bookseller's concentration on discount — until the mathematician became a retailer and spotted the hitch. The hitch is that, in real life, the range within which discount can vary is much narrower than the range of stock turn, sharply restricting discount's natural advantage.

Consider the experience at Under Cover Books. Discount ranged from a low of 34.11 percent to a high of 50 percent. Stock turn, on the other hand, ranged from a low of .08 to a high of 6.88 turns. The range between the high and low discounts in this real-life case was 47 percent; the range between the high and low stock turns was 8,600 percent.

The Case of the Balky Bookseller: A Hypothetical Single-Title Example

Would it surprise you to learn that a bookstore might sell twice as many copies of a bestseller as a comparable store, bought at eight points higher discount, and earn less profit? The following example is constructed here to demonstrate the power of stock turn over discount.

Let us consider a hypothetical experience with one title, a new publication called *The Case of the Balky Bookseller.*

The publisher's rep presents *The Case of the Balky Bookseller* to Bookseller A — A is for Able — and tells Able how wonderful the book is and how the entire country will go wild over it. And because the publisher is sure that any bookseller will sell 150 copies with ease, the publisher is offering a special discount of 48 percent — that's right, 48 percent — on an advance order for 150 copies or more.

Bookseller Able, no dumbbell, takes 150 copies at a discount of 48 percent.

The rep zaps the order to headquarters through his computer and goes on to Bookseller B — B is for Balky — who owns a bookstore of approximately the same size and general character as Bookseller Able. The rep makes the same sales pitch — but is shocked by the response.

Bookseller B balks. Sorry, no order for 150 copies. B is short of working capital, especially since the Random House rep has just left — with an order. Bookseller B has to work hand to mouth for a while.

Bookseller Balky says, "I'll take 25 copies, and reorder when I need more books."

Consternation.

"But I can't give you the special discount of 48 percent," the amazed publisher's rep pleads. "I can only give you a discount of 40 percent on 25 copies. At 40 percent, you only earn 66.7¢ on each dollar you invest (.40 divided by

.60). Bookseller Able, who took 150 copies, will be earning 92.3¢ on each dollar (.48 divided by .52). Bookseller Able will be earning almost 40 percent more than you do on every copy — and no matter how carefully you reorder, Bookseller Able will sell twice as many copies as you do, because Able is buying enough copies to make a display.

"You ought to know as a bookseller that it works that way every time — pile 'em high and watch 'em fly.

"Besides, if you don't buy better than that, we may have to transfer your account to our telemarketing department."

There was a lot more talk, but it didn't do any good.

Bookseller B, being Balky, would not budge from the order for 25 copies.

Under his breath, the sales rep said, "That's bookselling for you. You try to stuff money in their pockets and they fight you every inch of the way. There's no use arguing. They have to learn from sad experience."

In our story, The *Case of the Balky Bookseller,* it happened exactly as the publisher's rep had predicted. Bookseller Able sold every single one of the 150 copies over six months. Each dollar of inventory that Bookseller Able sold earned 92.3¢.

And Bookseller Balky sold only 75 copies — half as many as Bookseller A — and bought every one of those at the measly discount of 40 percent, earning only 66.7¢ instead of 92.3¢ per dollar.

What a difference between Bookseller Able and Bookseller Balky! Able earned a 48 percent margin on sales; Balky earned only 40 percent and, on top of that, Able had twice the sales.

The retail price of The Case of the Balky Bookseller is $20.00.

Bookseller Able earned 48 discount points on each copy ($9.60) times 150 copies, a total of $1,440, while Bookseller Balky earned only 40 discount points on each copy ($8.00) times 75 copies, or a total of only $600.

Bookseller A had double the sales and earned more money on every dollar of sales. Every accountant will agree — since profit is measured by margin against sales — that Bookseller A made a much higher profit, both in absolute dollars and as a percentage of sales.

Before any operating expenses, Bookseller Able earned $1,440 gross on sales of $3,000, or 48 percent, and Bookseller Balky earned $600 gross on sales of $1,500, or 40 percent. If that doesn't seem like much of a difference, consider that if operating expenses turned out to be 39 percent of sales, Bookseller Able earned $129.60 net (9 percent of $1,440) against only $6 (1 percent of $600) for Bookseller Balky.

Now let's look at the same *Case of the Balky Bookseller* another way.

Let's start by looking at a graph which summarizes how each of these booksellers bought *The Case of the Balky Bookseller.* This graph shows approximately how copies were supplied and sold in the two stores.

Bookseller Able started with 150 copies and sold them all over six months with no need to reorder. We know that the books do not sell down at a steady rate, so the straight line is probably not accurate. However, it is a reasonable approximation.

If the books were sold at the steady rate suggested by the graph, the average inventory was 75 copies over that period. If the title was eagerly awaited (a new Grisham or King novel, for example) and sold at a rapid rate to start and later slowed down, the average inventory was less than 75 copies (perhaps 60 or so); if, as is the case with far more titles, sales started slowly and speeded up as word of mouth developed, the average inventory was higher than 75 copies (perhaps 90). Since all we (you and I) know about this book is its title, we will assume that since Bookseller Able's 150 copies were sold in six

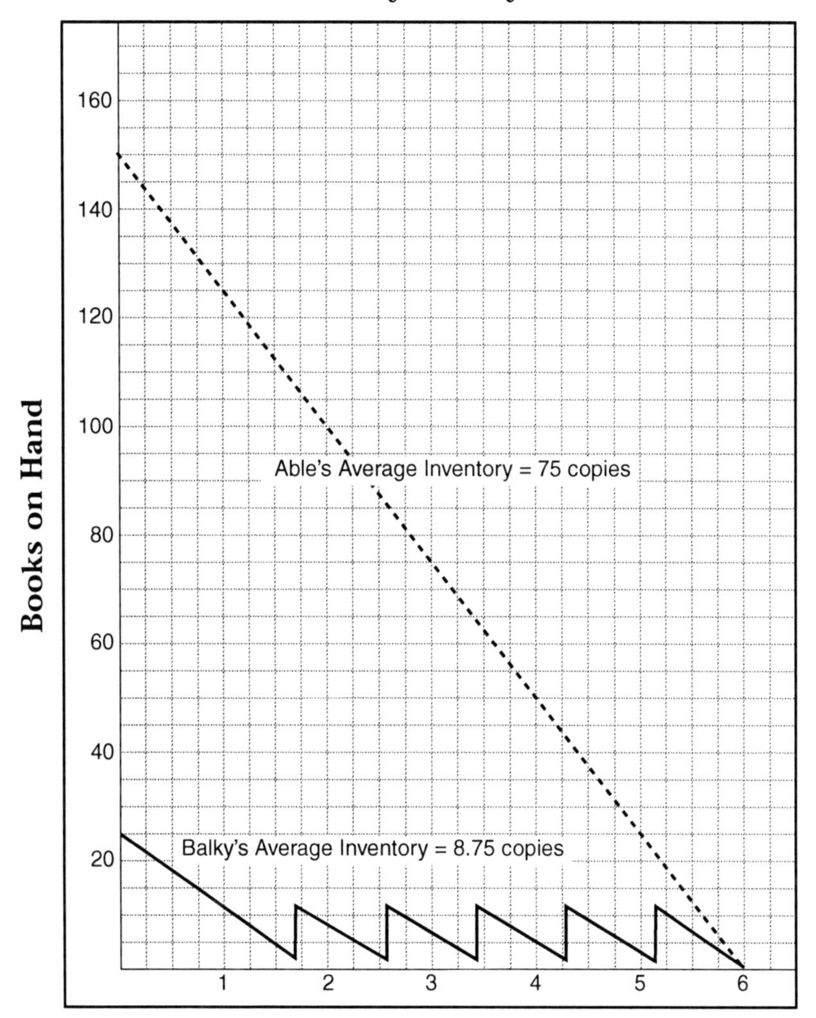

months, the average inventory was approximately 75 copies over that period. Therefore, on average, Able owned 75 copies at $10.40 per copy, and so had $780 invested in *The Case of the Balky Bookseller* during those six months.

Bookseller Balky, who did not pile 'em high, started with 25 copies and had a total sale over six months of only 75 copies, half as many as Bookseller Able. Bookseller Balky reordered ten copies every time the inventory hit two copies.

Buying six times instead of once, Balky carried an average inventory of 83⁄4 copies, compared to Able's 75 copies. On average, Balky owned 83⁄4 copies at $12.00 per copy, and so had $105 invested in The Case of the Balky Bookseller during those six months. Therefore, on average, Bookseller Balky had less than one-seventh as much money tied up in inventory on this title as Bookseller Able.

Dividing Bookseller Able's sale of 150 copies by the 75-copy average inventory shows two turns for the six-month period or a stock turn of four times a year.

Dividing Bookseller Balky's sale of 75 copies by the average inventory of 8.75 shows 8.57 turns for six months, and 17.14 for the year.

Let us see how that affects return on investment.

Bookseller Able, buying at 48 percent discount, earned 92.3¢ per dollar and earned it at the rate of four times a year, so Bookseller Able earned $3.69 annually per invested dollar on this title.

Bookseller Balky, buying at the low discount of 40 percent, earned only 66.7¢ per dollar, but earned it at the rate of 17.14 times a year, so Bookseller Balky earned $11.43 annually per dollar invested.

That's three times as much!

Let's look at an alternate way to compute this. As we noted, Able had an average of $780 invested in *The Case of the Balky Bookseller* and earned $1,440 on that investment in six months. Dividing the earnings, $1,440, by the investment, $780, tells us that Able earned $1.864 per dollar invested over six months, or $3.69 per year.

Balky's average investment in the book was only $105, on which Balky earned $600 in six months. A similar calculation tells us that Balky earned $5.714 per dollar invested in six months, or $11.43 for the year.

However you manipulate the numbers, the results are the same.

Bookseller Balky's earnings per dollar invested were more than three times higher than Bookseller Able's earnings. Balky did so well that Able would have had to buy at a discount of 74 percent, instead of 48 percent, to earn as much per dollar of working capital as Balky earned at 40 percent. (The calculation: the margin at 74 percent, .74 divided by .26, is $2.85, which, multiplied by the stock turn of four, becomes $11.40 return per dollar invested.)

Bookseller Able's high return on sales turned out to be a rather poor return on investment. Not only did Bookseller Balky earn substantially more on each dollar put into inventory, but Balky's average investment was one-seventh that of Able. Balky could handle seven titles like *The Case of the Balky Bookseller* (and be earning money from all seven) on the same average investment that Able needed to handle just one.

If Bookseller Balky invested in seven *"Case of"* titles, which Balky undoubtedly did, Balky's investment of $735 (at 40 percent discount) would have earned $4,200 against the $1,440 earned by Able's slightly higher investment of $780 at 48 percent discount.

This example could easily have been made more dramatic.

Look at that graph a little more critically.

If Bookseller Balky had been deliberately aiming at getting a high stock turn, the initial order would have been for fewer than 25 copies — say 20, or 15. And reorders, when the stock level dropped to 2, would have been for 8 copies or 6 rather than 10. That would have carried the title nicely without running out of stock or losing the 40 percent discount.

Balky's average investment would have been lower, the

stock turn would have been higher — and the return on each invested dollar would have been a lot more that $11.43

And that is not the only thing it might be worth changing in the plot of *The Case of the Balky Bookseller.*

There are two very serious things wrong with the scenario we've sketched.

First:

Is it really reasonable to expect that Bookseller Able would sell twice as many copies as Bookseller Balky just because Able piled the books high?

No one can doubt that better display sells more books. But any resourceful bookseller would get good display by making posters or using other physical props rather than piling up an expensive monument of actual copies of the title.

Even so, Able might get 10 percent higher sales — 20 percent — even 50 percent — but certainly not 100 percent.

Second:

If you can believe the Association of American Publishers (AAP), it would be very unusual if Bookseller Able bought 150 copies and did not return a single one.

AAP annual reports claim that about 30 percent of the copies shipped to booksellers are returned unsold. That is 30 percent of all copies shipped — advance orders, reorders, backlist, special orders — everything. Thirty percent of everything means, since approximately half the books shipped are backlist, at least 50 percent of new titles like *The Case of the Balky Bookseller* are returned.

But let's suppose that Able was luckier than the average — after all, the name Able should be worth something — and Able returned only 30 percent, not 50 percent.

So, in our example, Able would not look as able as we made Able look.

Able would have received 150 copies and returned 45 copies (30 percent), selling 105.

The average inventory over six months would have been the 52.5 copies from the 105 copies sold *plus* the 45 copies returned, or 97.5 copies total.

The stock turn for six months, instead of being 2, as we previously calculated, would actually have been 1.08, and the annual stock turn would have been 2.16, not 4.

Able's earnings would have been the 92.3¢ margin per dollar multiplied by the stock turn of 2.16, or $1.99 per dollar of investment, not $3.69 as we previously calculated.

It may seem reasonable, since Able made returns, to assume returns from Balky as well. But returns typically result from overbuying the initial quantity, as Able did. The bookseller who reorders five times in small quantities is not likely to make a return, although the last reorder may take a little longer to sell than earlier ones. If there were to be a return, it might be for one or two copies, which would not affect our example significantly.

Balky, even without improving the buying as we suggest Balky might have done, would have earned 5.74 times as much per dollar invested as Able. Able would have to buy at 84.1 percent discount to do as well as Balky did at 40 percent discount.

Let's consider what this exercise with numbers tells us about stock turn with respect to title spread and control of inventory. Bookseller Able stocked a bestseller and achieved a stock turn of four. Leaving aside discount — assuming that the bookseller bought all books at the same average discount — the gross margin earned per dollar invested was determined by the stock turn of four. Any title turning four times — whether it was a bestseller or a slow seller — would earn the same gross margin per dollar invested. Any title turning faster than four times would earn more gross margin per dollar invested.

So, for example, a title selling four copies a year, stocked at a level of one copy, would earn exactly as much per dollar invested as a title selling 300 copies a year, stocked at an average level of 75 copies. And if any title turns more than four times, whether the average inventory level is 1 copy or 75 copies (as Bookseller Balky demonstrated), it will earn more per dollar invested.

This suggests how much many booksellers can do — without increasing current investment in inventory by a single penny — to offer more titles, make the store more inviting and attractive, and increase sales and income.

We are still in the process of shaking the bookseller's faith in discount as the guide to business decisions — specifically, buying decisions. At the present level of maturity in our industry, this is the most important class of decisions the bookseller makes.

Discount is wonderful! We need discount. Retailing cannot do without it.

But *discount steps* are the Rhine Maiden of retail bookselling. Reaching for the next discount step can put buying strategy on the rocks of low stock turn.

Discount steps — even though they cost the publisher plenty — tempt the bookseller into wrong decisions. It is unfortunate that publishers have not figured out a more useful way to spend the money. The current trend to flat discounts is a step in the right direction, but it is only a step.

Stock Turn for the Entire Inventory: Another Hypothetical Example

We have seen how much more important stock turn is compared to discount on a single title. When a bookseller examines stock turn versus discount on the entire inventory in the store, the power of stock turn becomes even more evident.

Let's proceed from one specific title, *The Case of the Balky Bookseller,* to consider a store's entire inventory.

For example: if a store has an inventory of books worth $500,000 at retail, purchased at an average discount of 43 percent, the cost of those books (57 percent of retail) would be $285,000; if the entire inventory is sold, the 43 percent margin earned on it would be $215,000.

At one turn, total gross margin = $215,000;

at two turns, total gross margin = $430,000 (on the same $285,000 investment);

at three turns, total gross margin = $645,000 (on the same $285,000 investment);

at four turns, total gross margin = $860,000 (on the same $285,000 investment).

If the bookseller wanted to increase the gross margin at three turns ($645,000) to match the gross margin at four turns ($860,000), but wanted to hold the turn at three and simply increase the discount to reach the margin at four turns — the average discount would have to be raised from 43 percent to 50 percent. (At 50 percent discount, margin (.50 divided by .50) equals one. One multiplied by the stock turn of three, then multiplied by the investment of $285,000 equals a total gross margin of $855,000.)

In this situation, *one stock turn is worth seven points of discount.*

You can have a high gross margin of return against sales at the same time that you have a low gross margin of return against investment — and vice versa. That is because figures of gross margin are usually expressed as percentages, whether a percentage against investment or against sales. And percentages, unfortunately, can be misleading. Sales, for example, can never be higher than 100 percent — but the 100 percent can be a very different absolute quantity in two different cases.

Focusing on percentages can obscure what is actually happening.

Suppose your stock turn is increased and the result does not show any change in your gross margin percentage against sales at all — not even to the fourth decimal place. In fact, the gross margin percentage on sales may actually go down. It would seem that the stock turn increase has accomplished less than nothing.

But because the higher stock turn will have given you more sales than you would have gotten from the same inventory at a lower stock turn, your new percentage return on sales is calculated on higher sales. Your total gross margin on sales will go up even if your percentage gross margin hasn't changed — or even has decreased.

This can be seen very clearly from the above figures for a bookstore with an inventory of $500,000 at retail bought at a discount of 43 percent. The gross margin at one turn was $215,000 and at four turns it was $860,000. But the percentage return on sales, at 43 percent discount, remained 43 percent no matter what the stock turn. The 43 percent was calculated on a higher sales figure on a stock turn of four (to get a gross margin as high as $866,000) and a much lower sales figure at a turn of one (to get as low a total gross margin as $215,000).

It is obvious that even if the margin on sales went down from 43 percent to something less (42 percent? 40 percent?) because the discount changed, the total gross margin at a stock turn of four would still be dramatically higher than at a stock turn of one or two: another reason to beware of ratios and percentages.

Let's go from the hypothetical to the actual.

Schwartz Bookshops of Milwaukee: Real-Life Stock Turn Experience

A. David Schwartz of Harry W. Schwartz Bookshops made a comparative study of stock turn which indicated that the leverage of turn could make buying at a lower discount distinctly more profitable.

This example is from real life.

In October of 1981, *American Bookseller* magazine reported the results of a careful study by David Schwartz of the stock turn in his Milwaukee bookstore. Schwartz compared the turn on all the books in the store with the turn on just those books among them which had been bought from wholesalers. The across-the-board stock turn was 3.71, but on books bought from wholesalers, it was "more than double that figure." That means that on the books bought from wholesalers, the stock turn was 7.42 or more, while on books bought directly from publishers, the turn was actually somewhat less than 3.71.

Assume that the stock turn on books bought from publishers actually was as high as 3.71, and assume that all books bought from publishers were bought at a very generous discount of 46 percent. The margin at 46 percent discount (.46 divided by .54) is 85.2¢, which, multiplied by the stock turn of 3.71, equals a return of $3.16 per dollar, or $316,000 for each $100,000 invested in books bought from publishers.

On the other hand, even if the books bought from wholesalers earned only a 40 percent discount, so the margin (.40 divided by .60) was only 66.7¢, the stock turn of 7.42 resulted in earnings of $4.95 per dollar, or $495,000 for every $100,000 invested in books bought from wholesalers.

That little exercise showed that even at a lower discount — 15 percent lower in this case — the bookseller got over 50 percent more income from books bought from wholesalers (presumably in a pattern of frequent ordering of small quantities) than from books bought directly from publishers (presumably in a pattern of less frequent orders of larger quantities per title).

There is an interesting cash-flow aspect to David Schwartz's study of stock turn. At a discount of 40 percent and a gross margin of 66.7¢ per dollar, 30 days' sale covers the cost of the books at a stock turn of 7.2. Buying from wholesalers at a stock turn of 7.42 meant that the money to pay for the books came in (from the sale of those very books) shortly before Schwartz had to pay for them. In contrast, at the supposed 46 percent discount at which Schwartz bought from publishers, the stock turn would have had to be 6.48 (instead of the 3.71 actually achieved) to generate the cash in time to pay suppliers. (This is explained further in the next section.)

Of course, nothing magical happens to books that pass through the wholesaler's warehouse. You cannot distinguish a wholesaler-supplied copy from a publisher-supplied copy by heft or smell. The difference in stock turn that Schwartz discovered in the books in his store resulted from the fact that booksellers (Schwartz included) tend to buy smaller quantities of any title from wholesalers than they buy from publishers and to buy them more often.

If, as a practical matter, you could buy from publishers in the same pattern, publishers' books would reach the same stock turn. There would be other complications — many more packages, many more invoices to process, much more correspondence, for example — but the stock turn and the return on inventory investment would match those for wholesaler-supplied books.

Stock Turn and Cash Flow: Using Turn to Pay the Bills

Although striving for the highest possible stock turn is not recommended, the direct effect of turn on cash flow should not be overlooked. At some levels, stock turn can bring in sales income fast enough to pay suppliers for books when payment is due or even earlier.

When books which the bookseller bought at 40 percent discount are sold, 60 percent of the cash that comes in represents the cost of the books. The sales receipts, therefore, are 1.667 times (one divided by .6) the invoiced cost of the books; .667 of that is the gross margin.

If the bookseller pays suppliers, on average, in 30 days, a stock turn of 7.2 (.6 turns per month) will supply cash from sales just in time to pay the bills — a new interpretation of just-in-time buying. (If 7.2 seems a high turn to reach, just consider that Schwartz did a little better than that on purchases from wholesalers even without specifically aiming for high turn.)

If suppliers are paid in 40 days, a stock turn of 5.4 (.6 turns per 40 days) will do the trick; if suppliers are paid in 60 days, a stock turn of 3.6 (.6 turns in 60 days) is adequate.

Higher discount, on the other hand, is not very helpful in generating cash flow. At a 46 percent discount, the stock turn needed per paying period to meet suppliers' invoices from receipts declines to .54 from .6, only a minor improvement.

In all cases when the stock turn is sufficiently high to generate cash fast enough to pay suppliers for the books, the suppliers are financing the store's inventory. Applying buying methods aimed at improving turn can provide the cash to cover a steady flow of books and to have suppliers finance other operating expenses as well.

How the Earning Power of Inventory Declines: The Quiet Deterioration in Rate of Return on Investment

The longer you keep books in the store, the less they contribute to the rate of profit when they are sold. The decline in contribution to profitability begins as soon as the books arrive and is precipitous; the curve is a hockey stick.

The objective is to minimize the time between receipt and sale of any book. The easiest and least expensive way to sell books closer to the day they come in is to buy books closer to the day they are sold. Buying more often in smaller quantities is the least expensive and the most effective way to achieve that goal.

For a total sale of 100 copies, more will be sold within two weeks after they arrive if 10 copies are bought ten times than if 100 copies are bought once.

It matters much less how fast the title sells than how fast each investment in that title sells.

Below is a table that shows how much a bookseller makes at different discounts and at different sales velocities.

In this case, stock turn is interpreted directly (simply, as the time the books are in the store) rather than indirectly (dollars of sale divided by dollars of inventory), as the accountant usually does.

This tabulation shows how much the bookseller earns from each dollar of inventory investment, depending on the discount at which the books are bought and the amount of time the books spend in the store (the stock turn) before they are sold.

As the discount goes up, the bookseller's earnings go up; that is shown across the tabulation. As books wait in the store unsold and the dollars do not come in to be reinvested, the bookseller's annual return on those invested dollars declines; that is shown vertically.

Decline in Earning Power of Inventory Investment					
# of Weeks in Store Until Sold	*Amount Each Dollar Invested Is Earning Annually If Books Are Bought at Discounts Shown Below and Sold After the Number of Weeks in First Column*				
	40%	42%	45%	47%	Stock Turn
2	17.34	18.82	21.32	23.06	26.00
2.66	13.03	14.15	16.03	17.34	19.55
4	8.67	9.41	10.66	11.53	13.00
6	5.78	6.28	7.11	7.69	8.67
10	3.47	3.76	4.26	4.61	5.20
14	2.47	2.67	3.03	3.28	3.70
18	1.93	2.09	2.37	2.56	2.89
20	1.70	1.88	2.13	2.31	2.60
24	1.45	1.57	1.78	1.92	2.17
26	1.33	1.45	1.64	1.77	2.00
30	1.15	1.25	1.42	1.53	1.73
34	1.02	1.11	1.25	1.36	1.53
38	.91	.99	1.12	1.22	1.37
42	.83	.90	1.02	1.10	1.24
46	.75	.82	.93	1.00	1.13
50	.69	.75	.85	.92	1.04
52	.67	.72	.82	.89	1.00

Discount certainly does make a difference, particularly when one compares 40 percent discount with 47 percent discount. However, the tabulation shows at a glance that the time between acquisition and sale makes a much greater difference in the bookseller's income than difference in discounts.

Just in case this tabulation does not show you dramatically enough how quickly the productivity of inventory investment collapses as books spend more time in the store waiting for customers, consider the same numbers in graph form.

As you can see, the bookseller's investment goes bad almost as fast as the grocer's milk goes sour. The grocer has the advantage that the odor draws attention to the declining stock turn.

The graph indicates that stock turn is a powerful prybar for you to use to increase productivity of inventory investment; conversely, if you don't use it, circumstances will use the prybar against you to drain the productivity from your inventory.

Let's go back to our tabulation so we can use the numbers behind the graph.

Please note that this tabulation does not show how much any title actually earned when sold, but rather the rate — the annual rate — at which any title was earning and at which it was turning if bought at the discount and

Decline in Earning Power of Inventory Investment

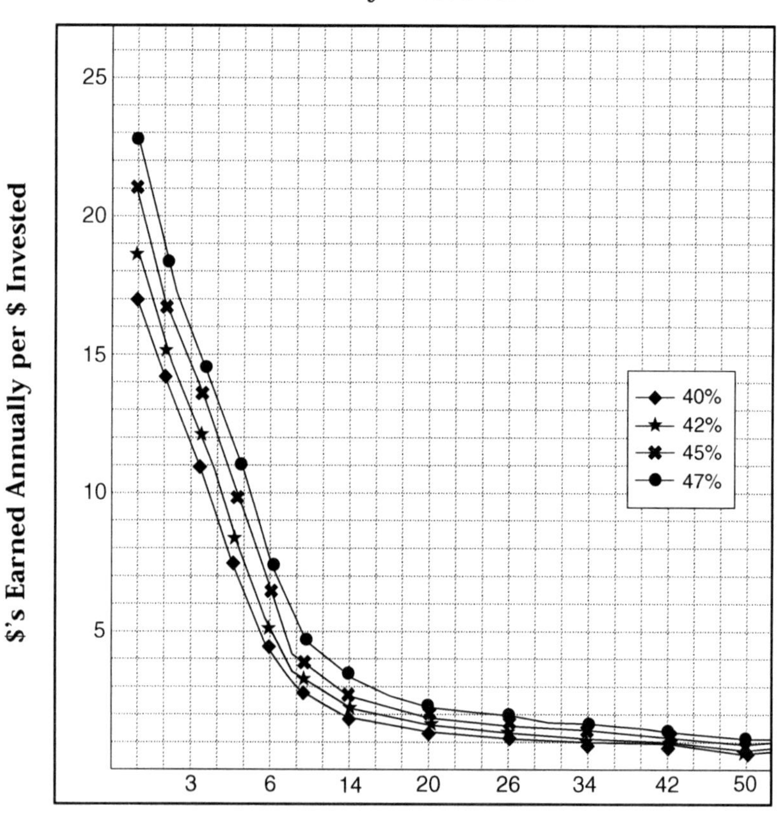

Number of Weeks in Store

sold after the number of weeks shown in the table.

Normally, we annualize these numbers — stock turn and dollars earned per dollar of inventory — so we can draw some useful conclusions.

For example, an accountant will tell you that your margin per dollar of inventory depends on the discount. At a discount of 40 percent, your margin is the discount, .40, divided by the cost, .60, or a margin of .66666, which we round off to .667. If you bought the book on January 2, that 66.7¢ per dollar is your margin, and according to your accountant, that margin stays the same whether you sell the book on January 15 or December 31.

But we know very well that selling the book on January 15, after it has been in the store for 2 weeks, is not the same as selling it on December 31, after it has been in the store for 52 weeks.

As our tabulation shows, if the book is sold after 52 weeks, the margin of 66.7¢ is earned only once that year so each dollar is earning margin at an annual rate of 66.7¢ per dollar.

If the book is sold after 2 weeks, one-twenty-sixth of a year, the dollar is earning at the annual rate of 66.7¢ multiplied by 26 — or at an annual rate of $17.34 per dollar.

Let's look more closely at a theoretical book that costs the bookseller one dollar (the retail price, at 40 percent discount, is $1.667) and examine the effect of the amount of time it takes to sell.

The book is purchased on January 2, and, if sold at full retail price, the margin per dollar of investment is $.667:

If sold on February 1, stock turn = 12 times annually, margin of .667 x 12 = **$8.004** annual gross income per dollar

If sold on March 1, stock turn = 6 times annually, margin of .667 x 6 = **$4.002** annual gross income per dollar

If sold on April 1, stock turn = 4 times annually, margin of .667 x 4 = **$2.667** annual gross income per dollar

If sold on July 1, stock turn = 2 times annually, margin of .667 x 2 = **$1.334** annual gross income per dollar

If sold on December 31, stock turn = 1 time annually, margin of .667 x 1 = **$0.667** annual gross income per dollar

Not only is the financial effect different if the book is sold earlier rather than later, but the difference is great enough to push the bookseller to go to some trouble and some expense to sell books closer to the day they come in.

The bookseller might invest in advertising over and above any publisher's co-operative allowance, or pay clerks an incentive bonus on sales, or offer customers a discount from the retail price — whatever, in the bookseller's judgment, would speed the movement of books out of the store, even if it involved some cost to do it.

But the surest and least expensive way to reduce the time any title spends in the store is to buy it in the smallest practical quantity as frequently as necessary. Of course, that will cost in discount and in clerical overheads, but those costs are minor compared to the cost of slower stock turn due to holding higher inventory relative to sales.

The tabulation also reveals that discount acts in a way not usually recognized. It is an anti-souring factor. Discount slows the aging of inventory. We have inserted a line in the tabulation for books sold at 2.66 weeks. If you look along that line, you will see that at 2.66 weeks, books bought at 47 percent discount earn exactly as much as books bought at 40 percent earn when sold after 2 weeks. That anti-souring influence is significant in the early period in inventory but becomes much less important as stock turn goes down.

So, the tabulation makes clear that discount does some good, but the effect is puny compared to buying more frequently in smaller quantities.

It must be emphasized that this tabulation tells you only what each dollar of investment will earn. It does not tell you what your calculation of the profit-and-loss percentage against sales will show. As you have seen from the examples of Booksellers Able and Balky, one has nothing to do with the other. And, as you now know, the profit or loss on sales is of questionable validity as a measure of business success.

Stock Turn: Is the Sky the Limit?

It has been shown that achieving a higher stock turn will deliver a higher gross margin on each dollar invested. However, the bookseller is interested not only in the *rate of profitability* — the percentage — but the *total dollars of profitability* as well. It may be that a larger total profit at a lower stock turn is preferable to a lower total at a higher stock turn.

What has been said about the relative importance of stock turn to discount may suggest that the higher the turn the better.

Of course, that is not true.

You can have a very high stock turn on a narrow assortment of titles — in other words, a high stock turn on a low investment — which will result in a low *total return on investment.* The total could be so low that you might not cover expenses, let alone make a profit.

One of the reasons for trying to reach a high stock turn is precisely to allow you to add titles — broaden the title assortment — and increase the total return on investment, while controlling the subsequent reduction in the rate of stock turn and the reduction in the percentage return on investment.

Let's illustrate what that means.

Going back to our example of the bookseller who had an inventory of $500,000 at retail, $285,000 at cost, for whom we were projecting stock turns of one, two, three or four:

Supposing, with a stock turn of four, that the bookseller decided the return on investment was high enough to justify additional investment. At a turn of four (and a 43 percent discount), each dollar invested in books was earning $3.02 on the average. Some books earned more, some less. The range might be (a guess) from $2.25 to $5.25 earned per dollar.

The bookseller might add titles — slowly and methodically, of course — to bring the inventory investment up from $285,000 to $385,000. The titles added would sell more slowly than the original titles; the stock turn would, therefore, drop, under the watchful eye of the bookseller, from four to, perhaps, three and one-half. At a stock turn of three and one-half (and the same 43 percent discount), the average earned per dollar of investment is $2.64, and the range might be from $2.00 to (the old) $5.25 earned per dollar.

The key, of course, in controlling this expansion of inventory breadth is how much an additional dollar invested results in additional costs. The cost of money may be 15 percent, and personnel and miscellaneous costs may add another 15 percent. The dollar of inventory which earns 30¢ is breaking even — it earns as much as it costs to have it there. In that case, the bookseller can afford to add to inventory — business logic might argue *should* add to inventory — until the next dollar earns less than 30¢.

If you divide the minimum acceptable earning level —

30¢ — by the earning in one turn at an average discount of 43 percent — 75.4¢ — you will see that 30¢ is earned at four-tenths of a turn. We suggested the stock turn after the expansion of inventory would be 3.5, which would be the average for all the titles with stock turns above and below that number. At an average of 3.5, it is very unlikely that any title would be as low as four-tenths.

Which brings us neatly to the next question. Just how broad should the store's inventory be?

Breadth of Inventory: How Many Titles Should You Have?

The bookseller must be concerned not only with buying most profitably title by title, but with how extensively the assortment of titles can be stretched economically. This is better decided by calculation than by gut feeling or some arbitrary numerical goal.

What is the right number of titles for the store? If some title level is right for Store A, is it also right for Store B; if it is right for January, is it also right for February, March, and April? If another store is opening in town, proudly proclaiming that it has 180,000 titles, should you have 181,000?

Of course, you would not logically start building inventory by arbitrarily determining some definite number of titles for the store. Ideally, you would include every title that fits the image you want to project for your bookstore, so long as that title would sell fast enough to justify the investment.

If the bookseller had absolute pitch — absolute *buyer's* pitch — the first title in the store would be the title with the strongest current sales potential. The second title would be the second strongest, and so on, to fill out the store's breadth of title assortment.

Where would you stop? Would you stop at a certain

number of titles or at a title with a certain sales potential?

There should be no disagreement on that. There is no arbitrary number of titles that can make any sense at all. But it makes a lot of sense for the bookseller to say, "I want to stock every title that brings in enough sales revenue to make its presence in my inventory financially worthwhile. I want to exclude only titles that earn less than that practical minimum."

Each bookseller may have a different idea of what minimum earning to accept.

Fair enough.

A high-rent, small-square-foot-area bookstore in a busy airport, paying high clerical salaries *should* have different stocking standards than a small-town, low-rent bookstore operated by the owner's family.

Supposing the bookseller decides that the minimum requirement for any title in the store is that the title earn a margin of 50¢ a year for every dollar invested in that title. Earning more than 50¢, the title goes in or stays in; earning less than 50¢, the title is passed over or dropped.

That is a very intelligent guideline for inventory construction and maintenance — but how can you use that guideline?

Another application of stock turn: Supposing our bookseller is buying at an average discount of 43 percent. That delivers a margin, as you may remember (.43 divided by .57), of 75.4¢ for each dollar. The margin drops to 50¢ when the stock turn (.50 divided by .754) drops to .66 times a year. According to this financial criterion, titles turning faster than .66 belong in the store; titles turning slower than .66 do not.

That's helpful, but the stock turn of any single title resembles somewhat the mean free path of any gas molecule — it may be .66 this moment, .72 the next, then .62, etc. The mean turnover — we don't suggest a "nasty" turnover, but the arithmetic mean — is .66, varying slightly from one moment to the next, and, as the physicist Heisenberg pointed out, not easy to measure.

We have a workable solution to that problem.

We are dealing with the slowest-selling titles, producing minimums in sales and margins. It is not particularly advantageous to deal with these titles individually — seems sort of silly, in fact. We can avoid Heisenberg's uncertainty principle and the skittishness of individual stock turns by dealing with these low-productivity titles in small groups.

In a bookstore with 15,000 or 30,000 or 100,000 titles, it seems reasonable to look at the weakest titles in groups of 100. Suppose the computer is asked to choose the weakest 100 titles in the store — it can do this through a simple program that ranks the titles in sales strength order and then lists the 100 titles counting up from the bottom. The stock turn of those titles would be calculated when the computer systematically does your other stock turn calculations (we suggest monthly). When the stock turn on the group fell to .66, those 100 titles would be dropped — they would be labeled "do not reorder" — not to be reordered when sold, even if any of them are sold, by chance, the very next day. As soon as one group of 100 titles reaches the "do not reorder" point, the computer would examine the next weakest 100 titles.

So stock turn can help the bookseller police the lower limits of the breadth of inventory assortment. You may decide to go beyond the economic limits — to build some kind of store image, for instance — but you owe it to yourself to know that that is what you are doing.

Caveat: I have to acknowledge a very serious problem for any independent bookseller dealing with the application of seemingly simple mathematics to any single title. That problem is discussed under the heading "Mathematical Prediction" later in this monograph, but the reader may have already spotted the difficulty in determining the stock turn on a single title, as described above, without using sales information collected from many stores.

Earning 50¢ per invested dollar — a stock turn of .66 — may be acceptable to the bookseller. A title is turning .66 times annually if, on average, it is sold 18 months after it arrives in the store. But a title sold after 6 or 12 or 18 or 24 months may be selling, in fact, at an average of 18 months — or at an average wildly higher or lower than 18 months. Without a great deal more data than the one sale in one store, we simply cannot know anything about the average.

Since the overwhelming majority of titles in any store are there in single copies (and, generally, more titles should be), detection of sales rates, trends, or stock turns, at least for those titles, must be based on sales data from many stores — data which, for the moment, are beyond the reach of any independent bookseller.

Breadth of Inventory: Where to Add Titles

Adding titles to inventory tends to lower stock turn. When the decision is made to add titles, the categories to be extended should be chosen by calculating which have higher turns. This will ensure that the assortment is broadened where customer interest is greatest.

If breadth of inventory is to be expanded by adding titles, where should they be added?

If you are calculating stock turn monthly — as you should — and doing it by subject category as well as by inventory overall, you will find that the turn varies, sometimes greatly, by subject category. If buying is catch-as-catch-can, a difference in stock turn among categories may indicate only some accidental differences in how books were bought, revealing nothing about the relation of breadth of stock to demand for books. However, if a sound buying policy is being applied and books are being bought frequently in small quantities, the stock turn in any category should indicate where adding titles is most likely to be advantageous.

For example, if the overall stock turn is four, but the turn in the biography category is two and in mysteries is eight, biography is distinctly less a candidate for adding titles than is mysteries. If the mysteries category can be divided further to see where the turn is greatest, that may pinpoint the subhead under mysteries that should get more titles. Even without subdivision, however, adding mystery titles in probable order of popularity should increase the total sale of books in that category while lowering stock turn.

Using the monthly stock turn calculation as a gauge to tell you when to stop adding titles will enable you to keep the situation under control. Categories that have a lower stock turn, like (in this case) biography, are by no means necessarily candidates for reducing the number of titles to increase turn. Controlling the lower limits of the inventory assortment is best left to the measurement of stock turn of the poorest selling titles overall. Broad inventory, including titles selling at turns below the average, acts to make the store more attractive and to help sell books in all categories. All titles cannot reach the highest turn, or even the average turn. Some slower sellers should be retained because they help sustain the image of a broad title assortment.

Second, sales in any category can be increased by offering more titles with no increase in inventory investment. This is done by replacing one title when it is sold with another. So, if one biography is sold, it may be replaced by another biography of the same person or one of a person associated with the subject of the sold biography. A list of titles that lend themselves to such "substitutability" should be identified in advance, and the computer programmed for the three or four titles in the sequence to be stocked before the original title appears again.

Decreasing stock turn *deliberately* to increase total gross margin is one thing — getting a lower stock turn *inadvertently* because you are chasing the higher discount is quite another. A sensible goal for any *title assortment* — not inventory investment — is to get the highest turn possible without running out of stock on strong titles.

Higher Stock Turn: Moving Toward That Goal

Most booksellers do not bother to calculate stock turn, so it seems odd to be promoting it as the guide for sound buying policy. Fortunately, improving stock turn is not as complicated a process for books as it may be for other merchandise. The key is buying more frequently in smaller quantities. That suggests a greater reliance on wholesalers.

If stock turn is so important, how do you get a higher stock turn?

Stock turn, after all, is not immediately apparent (like discount) when the order for the books is placed. Stock turn can be calculated only after the books are sold. What can you do at the earlier buying step that will assure a higher stock turn at the later selling step?

Some textbooks on retailing will tell you that you have to narrow down the spread of merchandise in the store — carry fewer titles — cutting out the ones that sell more slowly. This suggests that you have to accept lower income to get higher stock turn.

Don't you believe it!

That may be true for some types of retailers — but it

is not true for any bookstore we know about. If you are a superstore carrying 180,000 titles to prove you are macho or to knock out a competitor, the last 80,000 may not be doing your stock turn any good. But that is not where the problem of low overall stock turn lies with most booksellers. *Stock turn usually suffers because the bookseller does not use the leverage for higher turn inherent in the fast sellers.*

Just take a lesson from our Booksellers Able and Balky. Buy bestselling titles in small quantities — even smaller and more often than Bookseller Balky did — and your average stock turn will climb fast. Balky bought once a month and ran rings around Able. Any bookseller can buy more often than that.

Of course, every store is different and, in a practical sense, frequency of buying depends somewhat on the size and nature of the store; but, in my opinion, most booksellers can cover a major portion of their stock needs *buying daily* — mostly the bestsellers. Small stores may not be able to meet the wholesaler's minimum practical order requirement of 50 or 100 copies daily, and may prefer to buy every second or third day, depending on the season. The important thing is finding the shortest practical interval for orders for your store — and it may change from time to time.

Perhaps 95 percent of the titles in inventory are stocked in single copies, with that copy being sold, unpredictably, in three months or eight months or not at all. Daily buying skips almost all of those titles, because when one copy is on hand, no order is required. Such a title will only be included in the daily shopping list when that copy is sold, if then.

Although most booksellers buy every day, they buy for a longer term, tying up more money on each title than they need to tie up — thereby losing the advantage of buying every day. Buying the more active titles every day to meet *immediate* needs — only the quantities needed to avoid losing sales over the next few days, not the next few weeks — can do wonders for your stock turn, your working capital, and your cash flow. Buying every day can get you stock turns of 30 or 40 times on bestsellers with ease, and that can do a lot to bring up the stock turn across the entire inventory.

Buying every day probably means buying heavily or even entirely from wholesalers. We know now that the lower discount wholesalers usually grant is much less important than getting a higher turn and having more titles in stock. Also, having to pay more promptly — which is a drawback of buying from wholesalers — is easier to manage when high stock turns move cash into the store faster and in larger volume.

The bookseller's life is complicated enough, trying, as most booksellers do — for the sake of discount — to buy as much as possible directly from the publisher. Adding, on top of that policy, a strategy dictating "buy frequently in small quantities" in order to get a higher return on investment — and still buy directly from the publisher — could make those complications intolerable.

Going to the wholesaler to get a high stock turn and keep inventory investment low by ordering more often is appealing, largely because publishers have shown no appreciation of the advantage to the bookseller of that business strategy. Publishers — particularly the larger ones that have the capacity to be helpful — continue to press for turn-depressing advance orders in high quantities; they continue to restrict rep visits to once each publishing season; they continue to offer unpredictable (usually slow) fulfillment. More titles at the bookstore in small quantities is, actually, as much in the publishers' interest as it is in the booksellers'. Waiting for that realization to affect publishers' policies saddles the bookseller with the ongoing cost of low stock turn and high returns, so the booksellers will probably choose to buy from wholesalers rather than wait.

It is tempting to choose to buy everything possible from the wholesaler, placing orders daily or as often as the bookstore's size and the wholesaler's policies permit. If the buying shifts to wholesalers, as the economics seem to dictate it should, the publisher will be somewhat trapped. A bookseller who buys from a wholesaler needs as much or more attention from the publisher, not less. It is still essential for reps to call on the buyers to sell them on the merits of forthcoming titles (how else will the bookseller know what to buy from the wholesaler?), to pass along title information, to offer advertising allowances, to chat up the clerks, etc. The publisher still needs to know the store's inventory title by title, whether the information comes from an inventory tallied by the rep or through a direct connection between the bookseller's and publisher's computers, even though the order that results from that knowledge will be going to the wholesaler.

For new and forthcoming titles, a sensible buying procedure for a bookseller would be to have the publisher's rep present the new list, the planned advertising schedule, the author tours, and everything else the bookseller should know to anticipate demand — and then give the wholesaler an order for the number of copies likely to be needed to cover the initial uncertain selling period — say, two or three weeks.

Since wholesalers make it easy for stores to order frequently via modem, even smaller stores will regularly order the 100 assorted books that qualify for free freight from most wholesalers. With a greater volume of business, wholesalers will naturally broaden their title assortment even further — so that the percentage of the retailers' needs that require special orders to publishers should steadily decline.

One big advantage to the publisher, however, would be

that under distribution through the wholesaler in small, frequently dispatched quantities, returns and remaindering should drop significantly and the sale of mid-list and minor titles should increase markedly.

Buying Decisions: The Burden on Bookstore Management

The demands placed on management's time and attention by buying decisions tend toward a strategy of fewer and larger orders, in direct conflict with our desire to improve stock turn by more frequent smaller orders.

Buying decisions are the responsibility of bookstore management. It evolved that way because an essential responsibility of buying is *not buying* — foiling the pressure from publishers to put in excessive titles and copies. Under present conditions, the only way bookstore management can make buying decisions rationally is to consider the pertinent facts and decide, in its judgment, whether the title belongs in the store and should be ordered and, if so, how many copies.

The impossible demands these decisions place on management's time are made to seem possible — in large stores, bookstore chains, and wholesalers — by bucking decisions to enough individuals in lower levels of management to get the job done. Nevertheless, even in such cases, the costs in management time suggest that buying in single copies cannot, except for expensive books, be supported economically. It is true that advance orders are placed for single copies, but whether this is a reasonable use of the bookseller's and sales rep's time is sometimes openly questioned. Among the titles from forthcoming lists passed over by the bookseller, or not even presented by the rep, are many that could go into the store in one copy or two, but the lost sales resulting from their absence are considered an unavoidable "fact of life" under present circumstances. In addition, many titles are not reordered because the time and research necessary to reach a decision to order one copy or none do not seem worth it.

It is true that single copies certainly are ordered. A significant portion of these orders, however, are special orders—presold copies that represent no investment of management decision time and no inventory holding risk and are sold at the best stock turn possible: the bookseller has the money before the order is placed. Special orders suggest that there is more business out there, if only we knew what titles to stock in single copies so the books would be there to anticipate customer requests. Chains tend to solve the problem of wrestling with decisions to reorder in ones or twos for a large part of the list by overbuying, so reordering is necessary less frequently, and sometimes not at all. How long they can support the high cost of that buying strategy remains to be seen.

The inescapability of management's role, and the subjective, thoughtful manner in which that role is usually played, tend to push the buying pattern toward reducing the number of buying decisions — buying less frequently and in significant quantities. This is, generally, the bookseller's current buying stance. It tends to hold down the number of titles that can enter the book distribution system. More to the point, it conflicts directly with our conclusion that buying should be done frequently in small quantities for maximum profit. More frequent buying — thereby increasing the total number of buying decisions — would further strain, probably impossibly, the time and thought that management can invest in buying.

Consider a store with 30,000 titles and a stock turn of three. If all decisions were of the buy one or none variety, that would require something in the order of 90,000 decisions a year. Some decisions, even buying for immediate needs as recommended, would be for multiple copies, so perhaps only 80,000 decisions a year would be required.

But, if the buying strategy suggested here is applied, the 30,000 titles will quickly become 45,000 titles (actually cascading many more than that through the inventory), and stock turn is likely to be six or more. At a turn of six, even allowing for multiple-copy orders, a 45,000-title store would demand about 250,000 decisions a year, or about 1,000 every weekday for an average of 125 decisions every hour of an eight-hour day. The actual number would probably be higher to allow for the introduction (or rejection) of new titles and for the decisions not to reorder.

Since most choices will be between ordering one copy or none, and many titles will be in the five- to ten-dollar retail price range, many will be decisions on which the store cannot afford to spend more than fifty cents or a dollar of management time. Is it reasonable to expect responsible, well-compensated management to give each such decision serious attention, especially when, even if correct, many of these decisions would cost more in management time than they produce in margin on sales?

Buying Decisions: Subjective Versus Objective

Buying books is guided by an expectation that the books will be sold and the purchase is related somehow to that expectation. The expectation is usually subjective, but it can be an objective mathematical prediction. Where it can be applied, the objective approach offers distinct advantages.

Any decision by a retailer to buy *anything* is based on the expectation that it will be sold in some reasonable time frame. An *expectation,* whether or not one thinks of it in such terms, is at least a vague, subjective prediction that the item will be sold soon enough to make adding it to stock a sensible decision. The less vague and more precise, the less subjective and more objective that prediction is, the more useful it will be for making buying decisions. It is clearly not possible to *guarantee* that any item will be sold, and certainly not in some precise time frame, but it is possible to estimate the probability of sale — the odds that it will happen.

Estimating probability of sale can be done subjectively, and it usually is. The expert's mind sifts through some pertinent information or impressions — unconsciously, perhaps — and arrives at a "gut feeling" conclusion. Estimating probability can be done more objectively, however, by applying mathematical analysis to whatever information is available. If a computer makes the decision, it will be a formal arithmetic calculation, simple or involved, because for a computer there is no alternative to calculation — the computer does not know how to make a subjective estimate. The computer program explores the sales history to detect patterns that presage what the later sales experience is likely to be. There are various "statistical" methods for doing this; the one I used with great success at Doubleday in the mid 1950s is regression analysis.

Whatever method is used, there are at least three significant advantages to mathematical calculation over subjective estimates of probability. It is consistent: From the same information, the computer will deliver the same conclusion, no matter what the "predictor's" mood that day. Calculation can detect patterns from much less data, so decisions can be made earlier and changes in odds recognized more quickly. In addition, mathematical methods grade their own conclusions for reliability; each answer expresses, by the "standard deviation" or the "chi square" which accompanies it, how precise it can be considered to be.

Consistency is important, because it makes it possible to adjust mathematical prediction to a fine degree. There is not much use telling the human expert predictor, "You have been generally running five percent too high. Take a little off future predictions to allow for that tendency." But making such an adjustment in a mathematical procedure is no more complicated than hitting a couple of keys on the computer — and it works!

Being able to predict usefully with less information is an obvious advantage. The human, subjective predictor *does* "predict" with little, and sometimes with no information at all. There are many situations when there is no alternative because little information is available; but the "prediction" is more a guess than a prediction. Mathematical prediction can be applied earlier, on less data, with a higher degree of reliability.

Harking back to my Doubleday experience with regression analysis: Although the human subjective analyzers (a committee in this case) needed 60 to 70 percent of the advance sale to predict with useful accuracy what the final total would be (they did not actually know what percentage of the orders they had), we could supply more accurate mathematical predictions when as little as 2 to 5 percent of the advance sale was in. Since books had to be shipped close to publication date, printing decisions usually could not wait until 60 percent of the advance was sold, so subjective prediction was not only inferior; it was essentially useless.

The standard deviation feature of mathematical prediction is, perhaps, the most attractive. After the use of mathematics is established and decisions are routinely guided by calculation, it is certainly the most workable. The mathematical prediction that you will sell one copy of a particular title within the next 30 weeks may come with a standard deviation of two weeks; the prediction that a copy of another title will be sold within 30 weeks may come with a standard deviation of six weeks. Nineteen times out of 20, the mathematical rules state, the result will probably fall within two standard deviations above and below the prediction. In the first case, that range — for 19 out of 20 decisions — would be between 26 weeks and 34 weeks; in the second case, it would be between 18 and 42. Obviously, the data in the first case point more confidently to a prediction of 30 weeks than do the data in the second case. The standard deviation tells you how confidently you may act on the prediction — whether to put your money down or hold back.

It may be that there is not enough information to suggest a conclusion. More likely, the information is not internally consistent. If you look back to our data on discount and stock turn from Under Cover Books, you will see that there was just as much data in both cases (165 points), but (for very good reason) the data on discount did not suggest a pattern, whereas the pattern on stock turn would have been clearly evident from half the data.

Mathematical Prediction: One Store or Many

Although any objectivity in the use of sales data is desirable and improves decisions, actual prediction of future sales by title requires data from many stores. The value of having such sales information (currently routinely gathered in bookstore chains) is so great that a mechanism for gathering it among independents is likely to be created.

In the choice between subjective judgment and mathematical prediction, there is no contest. Mathematical prediction is preferable because decisions are better, and tighter control is possible. Just as important, mathematical prediction allows management to hand the ordering task over to the computer. In addition to all its other weaknesses, subjective judgment cannot be programmed into the computer, either to make the prediction of sale or to make the buying decision dependent on that prediction. Until objective information and rules can regulate sales prediction and the control of inventory, even the minor aspects of these activities will require the active intervention of bookstore management. Mathematical prediction will permit management to devote more time and attention to matters that deserve management attention.

There is one large hitch, however. Mathematical prediction needs information beyond the reach of any one independent bookseller, whose information consists only of the sales of each title in that store. Mathematics is not a crystal ball. To predict the future of any title, there must be enough data to detect, even by subtle means, a tendency in the sales history of that title. If all we know is that one copy has been sold — yesterday, last week, a month ago — we can make no mathematically defensible statement about what the sale is likely to be tomorrow. Yet, except for a handful of bestselling titles, this is all the information available on almost all of the titles in any single store. Even for the few bestsellers, sales in one store are too erratic and the life of many of these titles too short to permit useful prediction. For many titles, by the time enough sales data have accumulated to give the impression that prediction is possible, the selling life of that title is finished. Mathematical prediction based on sales data from only one store is simply not practical.

The situation is different if sales information is available from several stores, and different by orders of magnitude if it is available from many stores. Bookstore chains, for example, collecting detailed sales information daily from all their branches, have the capacity to predict very accurately, within small standard deviations, for most titles. Today, chains do not use that information for prediction, but accident or economic pressure will lead them to do it sooner or later.

Analogous gathering of sales information from many independent stores into a central depository available electronically for use by each participating store would enable independents to predict sales mathematically, title by title, and to control buying and book inventory with accuracy not possible from the data of one store. The advantages of having data from many, presumably somewhat similar, stores are immense. The most obvious advantage, though far from the most important, is that with data from one store, sales potential cannot be judged for a title that is not in the store. In the case of many stores, any one store does not have to assume the risk of introducing that title; its sales potential will be evident if other stores in the group acquire it.

If a store considers one copy sold every 6 months an acceptable level of sales to warrant retaining a title in inventory, an individual store cannot be sure, even after 9 to 12 months or more, whether a title meets that criterion; data from many stores can identify such titles in a week or two. Data from many stores can distinguish the salability potential among titles to a much finer degree than can data from one store. Since many thousands of buying decisions based on sales potential must be made over the course of a year even for a small store, the advantage is multiplied.

The substantial value of such information — depending on the number of independents involved, the advantages could run to millions of dollars annually — suggests that someone (an existing organization, a large bookseller, a large wholesaler, an outside business service) will come forward to organize the gathering of sales information to make mathematical prediction routine. When that happens, each bookstore, depending on the nature of its inventory assortment and of its customer traffic, would be able to select the most pertinent portion of the combined sales data and use it, probably daily, to predict sales on each title in that data pool and to guide ordering decisions, preferably according to rules entered into the computer. For titles in the store, ordering would only be considered when a copy is sold. For titles not in the store — perhaps because they were never bought in advance, perhaps because they were allowed to go out of stock because of low sales — ordering would be triggered when sales in other stores predicted an acceptable level for the future.

The key questions for each title in the sales prediction system would be: "Within what time period is the next copy of this title likely to be sold?" and "How many copies are likely to be sold in the next immediate period?" Those questions might be answered routinely for each title sold in each store daily as the new sales information is gathered.

The same prediction of sale could result in varying ordering responses from different stores, depending on their evaluation of their needs. For example, a store committed to maintaining a broad inventory would reorder titles that a store under different economic pressures and committed to a high stock turn would allow to go out of stock.

Buying for a Shorter Period: More Smaller Orders Rather than Fewer Larger Ones

There are distinct advantages — lower risk, more productive use of working capital, and overall control of buying — in aiming each purchase at supplying immediate rather than longer-term needs.

Whether buying is based on mathematical prediction, the gut feeling of an experienced expert, or any other system or lack of system, buying for a shorter period is less risky than buying for a longer period. Predicting or estimating or guesstimating the need for 2 weeks is more likely to be closer to the actual need than doing it for 20 weeks, or the life of the title. It is also less risky because the amount of money invested in buying for a shorter period is likely to be significantly lower — except in the many obvious cases where one copy will do for any foreseeable period.

Buying for a shorter period, because it reduces the commitment of working capital for any one title, makes it possible to represent more titles for any given total investment in inventory. If there was any doubt before about the advantages of broader inventory, it should have been dissipated by the distinct increase in sales demonstrated by the 100,000-title and 150,000-title chain superstores. While those numbers are probably exaggerated for public relations and to apply pressure on independents, the addition of legitimate titles has resulted in additional sales.

Spreading working capital over more titles, judiciously selected, results in more sales per dollar of inventory. And the higher stock turn implied by such buying makes borrowing to increase working capital a more practical possibility.

By increasing the number of decisions per dollar spent, buying for a shorter period results in two additional potential advantages. The larger number of decisions makes it more likely that they may be analyzed statistically — after the fact, of course — to search for ways to improve them. And the reduction of the amount of money committed to each decision and, therefore, in the cost of a buying mistake should encourage management to move toward routinizing buying decisions. This can be done by developing buying rules to be applied manually or by computer programs without human intervention. Either method would sharply reduce the administrative costs of buying and probably improve the results.

Reordering by Computer: Why the Idea Appeals

Reordering frequently in small quantities, as we recommend for maximum return on investment, multiplies the buying burden on management. That would tend to lower the quality of such decisions. Relief could be provided if the computer assumed part of the load; sales data exist in some degree for all reorders that could guide computer calculation of such orders.

As the bookseller moves toward a buying pattern intended to improve profitability — ordering smaller quantities more frequently — cost in management time of the smaller order will be harder to justify, and the increasing number of buying decisions will strain the capacity even of enlarged management teams. More and more, the choice will tend to be the ultimate for small orders — "buy one copy or none." And, as discussed previously, if the buying challenge is truly being faced, even a modest bookstore will be presenting that choice about 125 times an hour.

That prospect argues strongly for exploring the possibility that computer programs might make at least some of those buying decisions at a cost of pennies rather than dollars, and with zero strain. Some small part of the benefit might be the likelihood that the computer would recognize much more quickly and surely than a human being the "repeats" in the 125 hourly situations, where the titles differ but the data are essentially the same.

If the computer cannot assume part of the buying load, the strategy of buying frequently in small quantities probably cannot be successfully applied — at least, without nervous breakdowns at management levels. Without belittling the complexity of the bookseller's buying responsibility, however, there are strong indications that some of that burden *can* be shifted to the computer.

If the buying rules in any store or group of stores are to be applied consistently — where the same prediction of sale against the same inventory background will result in the same decision — the situation is ideal for computer application.

Forty years ago, the Doubleday Merchandising Plan "ordered" books into hundreds of stores manually but used computer "logic" to make the decisions with no "buyer" interference. It increased the stores' profit on Doubleday books dramatically. Based on that experience and the natural logic of the situation, we are of the firm opinion that ordering based on computer decision will produce more profitable results than ordering by management decision.

Perhaps that is too romantic a notion. But there seems to be no way that bookstore management can take upon itself the responsibility for such a large number of low-value decisions. The only way to truly buy frequently in small quantities is to lighten management's load by turning over a portion of those decisions to the computer. It seems likely that the computer can make all the *reordering* decisions, for which sales histories exist, leaving the initial, advance buying to management.

It is definitely not suggested that computer programs such as those presently incorporated in any of the commercially available "inventory control" systems (e.g., IBID or WordStock) can make useful buying decisions. Whatever the merits of the logic on which these programs are based, their "decisions" apply only to the small percentage of titles (two percent? five percent?) selling fast enough and long enough in any one store to create a computer-recognizable pattern from which future sales can be mathematically projected. In addition, these inventory control systems are based on the application of current strategies aimed at infrequent — certainly not *daily* — buying. The unreliability of these buying programs is underlined by the fact that their sponsors uniformly suggest that the computer's "recommendations" be reviewed by management, which is akin to asking management to invest the time to go through the entire analysis required to decide an order in the absence of a computer — the saving in management time and assistance to management judgment being just about zero.

The goal of true computer ordering should be, given the titles management decides should be represented, to achieve the highest possible stock turn with a minimum incidence of being out of stock on better selling titles, and with a minimum commitment of management time.

A properly conceived computer program would avoid the impossible requirement that each decision be reviewed by management. The objective is not to review the *decisions,* but, rather, to review the *decision rules.* Is the computer program, applying those rules, making the best possible buying judgments? The results of a series of decisions would suggest when and in what way the computer program could be improved. Corrections could be introduced by management or could be applied continuously by the computer itself. Since almost all decisions would be to buy one copy or none, the financial risk from a single wrong decision would be trivial. Looking at the pattern of decisions would, in any case, be much more rewarding.

If the computer is to do the ordering, it should be provided with rules that create an order aimed at high stock turn, and the order should be forwarded to the supplier without management review. Properly programmed, the computer can continuously review and grade its own work and adjust the rules to improve results on subsequent orders.

Reordering by Computer: How the System Might Work With or Without Prediction

This is not the place to develop finished specifications for a computer reordering system. Such a system will require months of planning and experiment and will have to prove itself, in any case, by running parallel with manual buying by management. However, defining the nature of such a system can be a start toward its development.

The computer can function only if the operating instructions are clear and unequivocal. For any set of circumstances — inventory on hand, sales this week, sales last week, etc. — there must be one and only one clear conclusion: to order or not to order and, if yes, how many.

Ideally, sales information from many stores would provide data for a mathematical prediction of sale for each title as the title came up for consideration. That prediction, weighted by the relative size of the standard deviation (which indicates the reliability of each prediction) and the inventory on hand, would determine the ordering decision. Whenever a book is sold, the computer would consult the sales information for that title and calculate a prediction of sale to determine whether a reorder should be placed.

Where sales information from other stores is not available — currently true for all independents — and valid prediction is not possible, the buying decision would be based on current inventory and the sales experience of that title in that store. The sales experience in one store cannot produce a prediction, but it can provide an understandable computer instruction, which is a poor but useful substitute. For active titles, the computer might use the sales data for the preceding several days; for the great majority of less-active titles, the computer might refer back to the most recent sale, or, if this was the first sale, to the date of acquisition. That is more properly a *projection* rather than a *prediction.*

Whichever method is used, the computer would allow for seasonal bias — tennis, skiing, general travel, children's, Christmas titles, graduation gifts, etc. — programmed to raise or lower order quantities to correspond to the season. Orders placed for textbook use, an author appearance, or any special sale would be coded to put them outside the computer's normal calculations. And, of course, management would be free to place any order — advance order, special order, or order on a whim — or make any return without reference to the computer decision rules.

That, broadly sketched, is the way the development of a computer reordering program might be approached. The basic rules would be installed in the initial program and then fine-tuned by actual experience. Adjustments to the program could be made by management reacting to the program's performance, or the computer could adjust itself, or the two approaches could be combined.

The computer has the distinct advantage over human buying judgment in that the computer can survey its work for the previous period and play "what if" games, with variations of the decision rules determining what changes would have improved the outcome — and then changing the rules accordingly. There can be as many different sets of rules as there are stores. Rules would be constantly revised and improved, based on actual results. The important thing is to cast the rules in such a form that the computer can apply them automatically, without appealing for human interpretation. A concrete example, although the numbers are completely arbitrary and not intended to be taken seriously, may clarify how a computer reordering system might work. If sales prediction is based on data from many stores, a sample set of rules to determine whether or not to order, activated whenever a copy of any title is sold, might be something like this:

- If the prediction is for sale of one copy or more over the next 5 days, order enough copies to bring inventory to three times the prediction, rounding up from one-half copy. If inventory is at that level or higher, do not reorder.
- If the prediction is for sale of less than one copy over the next 5 days, but for one copy or more over the next 20 days, order enough copies to bring inventory to twice the prediction, rounding up from one-half copy. If inventory is at that level or higher, do not reorder.
- If the sales prediction for the next 20 days is less than one copy, and if any sale is predicted over the next 6 months, order enough copies to bring stock up to the level of predicted sale, rounding down from one-half copy. If inventory is at that level or higher, do not reorder.
- If no order is placed based on a 6-month sales

prediction, and if any sale is predicted over the next 12 months, order to bring stock up to predicted level, rounding down from one-half copy. If stock is at that level or higher, do not reorder.

- In all other cases, do not reorder.
- For any titles not currently in stock, if the system predicts that one copy or more would be sold in the next 20 days, order one copy. Thereafter, when that copy is sold, the stock level for that title is controlled by the preceding rules.

Such rules can work, however, only if the computer has the sales information from many stores continuously supplied to it. For stores with no information other than the history of sales in that store, such an ordering strategy cannot be applied because prediction is not possible. Yet, it is extremely desirable to order frequently in small quantities and control ordering by a consistent set of rules applied by a computer without management involvement in each decision. In those cases, although it is not nearly as solid a basis for ordering decisions, the date of the previous sale of any title can control the decision whether or not to order and can do so through a computer program. Such a program would, at least, have the advantages of consistency — essential for control and adjustments to the program — and of shifting title-by-title buying from bookstore management to the computer.

A possible set of rules for operating such a one-store ordering system might look something like this:

• If the previous sale of the title (or its acquisition) was x or more weeks ago, do not reorder.

• If the previous sale was between x and y weeks ago, bring stock on hand up to one copy (no reorder if present stock is one copy or more).

• If the previous sale was between z and y weeks ago, bring stock on hand up to two copies (no reorder if present stock is two copies or more).

- If the previous sale was c days to z weeks ago, bring stock on hand up to three copies (no reorder if present stock is three copies or more).
- If previous sale was earlier than today but later than c days ago, bring stock up to four copies (no reorder if present stock is four copies or more).
- If today's sale was two copies, bring stock up to six copies (no reorder if present stock is six copies or more).
- If today's sale was more than two copies, bring stock up to three times today's sale (no reorder if present stock is three times today's sale or more).

This explains how the bookseller might use the computer to decide whether to reorder and how many copies.

In addition to determining what books to reorder, the computer must direct the orders to the proper suppliers. That will depend, in the first place, on management's preferences — which publishers to favor by direct buying, how much to use wholesalers and which ones, etc. — and the initial order-routing program will be written accordingly. However, the mathematics of gross margin return on inventory investment, pushing for small orders frequently placed, will tend to increase the use of wholesalers, except for the larger publishers by the larger bookstores.

Orders would be electronically routed to publishers or wholesalers by most advantageously balancing speed, discount, freight costs, and even such factors as the experience with that supplier in accuracy in fulfillment and the incidence of damaged books.

For example, the rule for (large) Publisher A might be: if the number to order reaches ten assorted within two days of the first copy on the reorder list for Publisher A, the order goes to the publisher; if not, at the end of the two days it goes to the wholesaler. For (smaller) Publisher

B, the rule might be five assorted within three days. These are rules the computer can handle with ease.

The natural trend toward increased buying from wholesalers might be accelerated by negotiating improvements in their service. Some helpful changes might be the expansion of title assortment, lowering the minimum order for free freight, allowing discount for prompt payment according to number of days from delivery instead of the day of the month, packing books for easier store placement, and so on. If the sales information network is established to use sales prediction to guide reordering, wholesalers could use that information to have the right titles on hand when they are needed.

Advance Ordering: Getting Tighter Control

While reorders have some background sales data to serve as a guide, advance orders have none. Some authors have a sales record so consistent that a repetition of the previous title's sale, particularly over the first two weeks, can be assumed, but they represent only a tiny fraction of each year's output. Advance ordering cannot rely on title-specific sales data.

We have been discussing reorders, the supply of copies of titles for which there is some sales experience to guide the ordering decision. Considering whether or not to buy is governed by actual sales experience, and the decision is guided by what the sales data indicate about future prospects. But for titles ordered in *advance of publication,* no sales data of any sort exist. Though the advance order must, therefore, bypass any computerized reordering procedure, it must not be completely random.

The advance sale does not serve the same function for the bookseller as it does — or as the publisher may imagine it does — for the publisher. The publisher may aim for large numbers for internal political reasons, or to impress the buying public, or to justify a large enough printing to achieve a low "unit manufacturing cost," or for some other rational or not so rational reason.

The advance purchase, for the bookseller, has a simple and straightforward function. It is to keep the title in stock from the point at which no sales experience exists — the evening before publication day — until actual sales (or their absence) provide solid information on which to base the store's buying decision for that title. An advance order substantially larger than that quantity — for example, to get higher discount or more impressive display — is likely, as Bookseller Able discovered, to be extremely costly. It may not be clear how to determine that quantity precisely, but the *aim* of determining or approximating that quantity should be amply clear.

Depending on the title and the flow of sales information, a sales trend may be detected relatively quickly. It may take no more than two or three days, and for a bookseller with a reliable wholesaler source, that will be long enough for reorders to arrive on time. Because we are dealing with gross approximations and the cost of the safety factor is minor, it seems wise to aim the advance order to hold the store for a longer period — say, two weeks. Planning for two weeks is likely to produce orders lasting three days to four weeks or even longer, and that is an acceptable improvement over present experience.

Predicting the need for the first two weeks should be less wide of the mark than attempting to predict for an indefinite period or for the life of the title. Still, some guidance, in addition to intuition and the publisher's hype, would be helpful.

That guidance can be provided by history. Since none of the titles on this season's lists appeared on last season's or last year's, we cannot use any previous title as a guide. Because the times are different, even if an exactly comparable title was published on a prior list, the response to this title cannot be inferred by the response to that. But, even though each title is different, the distribution of sales levels among the titles, particularly over a narrow two-week span, is not likely to be wildly different from previous experience.

A profile of the sales history over the first two weeks of the titles on previous lists — the percentage that sold more than x, the percentage between x and y, etc. — can guide the bookstore buyer in assigning order quantities to the titles on present lists. Previous profiles should not be followed slavishly; they are rough guides, but extremely helpful if used in that way.

By assuring that response to strong sales will be reliable and swift, the computer reordering system, when it exists, should help management, which cannot shed responsibility for advance orders, resist the temptation to overbuy. For buying in advance, it is useful to divide titles (by management judgment) into two groups: immediate response titles and delayed response titles.

Immediate response titles are those for which some sales activity is expected soon after they go on sale. Wide sections of the public are aware of these titles, and they are likely to get heavy review attention and/or to be heavily promoted by the publisher. The number of copies ordered may be several or only one, but some sale is expected within the first two weeks that copies are in the store.

Delayed response titles are those which should be in the store's inventory assortment but are not likely to be sold quickly. Such titles are likely to be ordered in ones, to be reordered, if necessary, according to the computer reordering rules; the one copy purchased in advance may be sold unexpectedly the first day or, perhaps, not for six months.

The rules governing computer control of reordering will kick in the moment each title ordered in advance is placed on sale. Each title's sales history starts the moment the title reaches the store and the computer can start applying rules. The advance order, based on human judgment without computer help, should not create conditions that undermine the effectiveness of computer reordering. This first order should aim to put in initial inventory *only* as many copies as necessary to meet the first surge of demand and to stay in stock during the few days it takes the computer system to take hold.

Aiming the advance order to cover the possible demand over the first two weeks should improve stock turn by underbuying strong titles (by present discount-driven standards) with the confidence that the computer reordering system will keep them in stock. At the same time, advance ordering can encompass more titles, because buying immediate response titles in this manner will make more working capital available for advance buying generally.

Delayed response titles will typically be bought in ones, rarely twos. Being too cautious about such titles may result in lost sales for unstocked titles that might have been purchased by customers. Perhaps even more damaging, by reducing the store's attraction to the book-buying public, it may also cost sales of titles actually in stock to potential customers who were never enticed into the store. Being more daring — representing more less-active titles — will risk the clerical cost of making returns. Prediction based on multistore information will spot the candidates for return long before the publisher's return deadline. (You can see that we are assuming that such multistore information systems will be developed for independent booksellers.)

The advance order should be the maximum quantity expected to be sold in the first two weeks. In the case of delayed response titles, the one copy bought in advance may not be sold for six or eight months, which would still be within the acceptable range of stock turn.

Reordering by Computer: Policing the Results

Even in a relatively small bookstore, a well-designed computer reordering system will be making buying decisions involving risks too small to warrant management policing, and, in any case, too numerous to permit individual study. It is the overall results, rather than the individual buying decisions, that need to be policed.

One clear advantage of a computer-directed ordering system — even an extremely rudimentary one — is that it lends itself easily to policing and correction.

Actually, this "policing and correction" is integral to the initial development of the computer system itself. The ordering results must be measured, frequently at first, and adjustments made to correct the unforeseen errors and omissions inevitable in starting such a radical departure in inventory management. It would be amazing if these procedures could all be correctly determined a priori.

Even after the system is debugged, it should be periodically or continuously examined and corrected. Whether management intervenes to make the corrections (as it must in the early debugging process) or has the computer correct itself, the results of the computer's buying decisions must be used to determine what adjustments are desirable.

The performance elements to be policed are essentially the same whether the system is based on prediction from multistore sales information or projection from data of previous sales in one store. In general, no matter how long the system has been in operation, the possibility for improvement is always there. However, since even the most carefully conceived and operated system deals with approximations — made more precise all the time, it is to be hoped, but still approximations — corrections aiming at too much precision can give the computer a nervous breakdown.

For policing the computer's inventory control performance, it is useful to distinguish between more-active titles, which deserve closer attention, and less-active titles, which can be treated more routinely. In order to operate differently on titles designated as "more active," the computer must have some way of identifying them. The best definition, easily grasped by the computer, would be titles that are in stock in quantities greater than one. That definition may include some borderline titles, though it should be anticipated that, with daily ordering minimizing the cost of being out of stock, a larger percentage of titles than at present will be represented in single copies.

How often are more-active titles out of stock? (The less-active titles can be ignored for this purpose. Among the titles in the store in ones, having this or that one out of stock will not be unusual, and no sensible attempt can be made to avoid or minimize it.) With respect to more-active titles, the broad performance targets can be set by management. An airport bookshop, in which customers do not special order books or do not come back to get a title they failed to find initially, will aim at a lower incidence of out-of-stocks than a neighborhood store, where customers are more inclined to wait one or two days to get the title. But if active titles are *never* out of stock, the system is delivering a lower stock turn than necessary. The correction may be found in the reorder rules (reordering too soon? reordering too many?) and/or in the more subjective advance ordering (change ordering target to one week's supply?).

Can more titles be added in the acceptable range of return on investment? In what subject categories? Can overall turn be improved without loss of sales? That is another way of asking whether inventory investment can be reduced without measurably increasing out-of-stocks.

Bookstore management must decide again and again what it wants the system to accomplish, because the objective can become more ambitious as experience demonstrates how much the computer makes possible. But, even though they change from time to time, the criteria must be determined by management.

If the computer is to self-police the system — which we believe it can do more effectively than the cleverest bookstore management — it can be programmed, for example, to examine performance before and after the most recent 20,000 purchases (perhaps more for a larger store). The computer can compare the actual results, both on the active titles and on inventory overall, with those results that would have obtained if different buying rules had been guiding those 20,000 orders. If any alternative set of rules would have improved results by some minimum percentage, the computer can change its own rules automatically.

The reason for requiring a minimum improvement to change the system's rules is to avoid the effect of chance factors that can make the same set of rules accidentally more or less effective from time to time. That minimum should be greater than the range of chance factors. Chance will be much less a factor in prediction systems using data from many stores than in projection systems based on one store's data.

The entire purpose of applying mathematics to bookselling is to reduce the degree to which chance influences the operation of a bookstore — to bring bookselling under a greater degree of control. Whenever mathematics (or, if you prefer, logic) can be brought to bear, improvement in performance is likely to result.

In this discussion of discount, stock turn, and the strategies of buying and stock control, we have ignored two very timely bookselling problems that can benefit from a mathematical overview — returns and discounting.

Returns: Distinguishing between the Very Valuable Right to Return and the Very Costly Returns Themselves

The right to return unsold copies is probably the most salutary development in the history of American publishing. However, publishers, who created that right back in the 1930s, have encouraged its corruption to produce returns at catastrophic levels, for which they wrongly blame booksellers rather than their own aggressive unrealistic selling. In fact, returns are more costly to the bookseller than to the publisher.

Today, when publishers are complaining loudly about booksellers' profligacy in buying and then returning huge quantities of unsold copies — about half the newly published titles shipped to the stores — it might be appropriate to point out:

- There is a very meaningful distinction between the *right to return,* which is the publisher's sort of "manufacturer's guarantee" that the order being pressed upon the bookseller is sensible and safe — and the actual *returns,* which (at current ridiculously high levels) demonstrate that those orders are not really sensible and safe.
- The right to return was created *by* the publishers and for the publishers, and the surest way for a trade publisher to put itself out of business is to cancel that right.
- Returns are created *by the publishers themselves* when they press the booksellers for high advance orders, using sales pitches and inducements that the publishers will have forgotten when the inevitable returns start to arrive.

- Returns cost the bookseller much more than they cost the publisher.
- A substantial portion of returns are phony, comprising additional prepublication copies that publishers thrust upon the chains, because the publisher's co-op advertising formula calls for more copies to be bought than anybody reasonably expects to sell. Both parties know these books are in temporary residence.

The right of the bookseller to return unsold copies was invented by American publishers during the depression of the 1930s. In those days, booksellers had difficulty finding enough money to pay their rent. The right to return was intended to induce them to continue investing in inventory. It certainly worked. It marked the beginning — long before shopping malls and Wall Street money underwrote chain-store expansion — of a steady growth in the network of bookstores throughout the country.

The right to return, reducing the bookseller's anxiety in making the store's book assortment broader (and, unfortunately, deeper as well), was not intended to actually encourage returns. It was offered to make booksellers more relaxed in making what publishers regarded as fairly safe buying decisions. As it has been used by publishers' reps (with strong encouragement from the home offices) to pump up order quantities on lead titles, effectively reducing representation of lesser titles, the *right* of return has become more and more the *ritual* of return.

The approaches to buying we recommend here for booksellers are likely to reduce the rates of return to a trickle while extending the breadth of title assortment. But, in the meantime, returns are a real problem for bookstore management — the obvious problem of books being sent back on titles that were overbought, and its not-so-obvious silent partner, sales lost on titles that were underbought or skipped to forestall possible returns.

As most booksellers are well aware, and as the Association of American Publishers annual reports show, the rate of returns has been climbing steadily over the past 10 or 15 years. Publishers almost unanimously blame booksellers, sometimes very loudly, claiming that booksellers allow themselves to be lax and irresponsible because the publisher is the only one at risk.

The publisher is *not* the only one at risk. It is the publishers who, by their selling methods, create the returns risk and the actual future returns. But, in fact, the cost of returns falls much more heavily on booksellers than it does on publishers.

To start, the bookseller usually pays the cost of shipping all of those excess books into the store, of unpacking and accessing them, of corresponding with the publisher to get permission for the return (if necessary), and of packing them for return and shipping them back to the publisher.

But these nuisance problems and costs, including clerical and executive time as well as out-of-pocket expense, will probably amount to not more than five or six percent of the actual value of the returned books. At a return rate of 20 percent, these costs add up to about one percent of the total cost of the store's purchases.

Not so bad.

Now let us look at not-so-obvious costs.

The bookseller's most valuable business tool is *working capital* — the money the bookseller invests in book inventory to convert back into more money. The effective use of that working capital is the key to success in retailing books. Books that are returned — even if every penny is recovered from the publisher with a minimum of hassle, which very rarely happens — represent an investment of working capital that does no work. It is the equivalent of the bookseller taking money that would have produced sales and generated margin on sales, tying up that money securely in an old sock and stashing it under the mattress.

For a retailer who is borrowing money (at interest) to finance his or her book inventory — and a well-managed bookstore would certainly be doing that — the incipient returns represent money under the mattress on which interest is being paid. For the period that the books are held (and the additional time it takes the slow-moving publisher to process the return and issue the credit), the one percent cost of returns is increased by the interest paid on nonproductive money.

The publisher may be quick to protest that, judging from the mammoth size of its accounts receivable, the bookseller delays payment to the point that the publisher is acting as banker at zero interest. To some extent, varying with the publisher and the bookseller, such "borrowing" does take place. To that degree, the money under the mattress is not costing interest — just productivity. But that avenue of "borrowing" is limited, and the credit advanced by the publisher could be better invested in the titles of that publisher that are selling instead of extra copies of titles that are not.

But returns cost the bookseller more than the simple cost of interest or the better use of credit. Stock turn — the number of times each year a dollar invested in book inventory is sold and reinvested — is, as we now well know, the measure of how well the bookseller's working capital is working. If the stock turns three times a year in that store, the total annual sale at cost equals three times (300 percent of) the average investment in inventory. At a stock turn of three, every dollar of returns represents three dollars of lost sales at cost. If the average discount is 43 percent, every dollar of returns represents a loss in net income of three times 75.4¢ (.43 divided by .57), or $2.26. And, if the bookstore is making a profit or breaking even, that $2.26 would have gone right to the bottom line; it represents pure profit unadulterated by any cost except taxes.

Or, look at it another way.

Assume that returns represent 20 percent of purchases. In order to sell 300 percent of average inventory (our stock turn is three), the bookseller must buy 375 percent, because 75 percent (20 percent of 375) is returned. In effect, since the returned books are not "stock turning" at all, the 80 percent active investment which does produce sales is actually turning 3.75 times (80 into 300 is 3.75) to make it seem that the stock turn is three.

Suppose the bookseller sells everything that is bought, instead of just 80 percent. That would increase the total annual sale (at cost) from 300 percent of inventory investment to 375 percent of the same average inventory.

We'll assume that, buying at an average discount of 43 percent and selling 80 percent of purchases, the store covered all fixed costs (rent, light, salaries, etc.) — and produced a profit of 10 percent on sales. If the store's profit was 10 percent of sales and the discount was 43 percent, the cost of everything except the books was 33 percent of sales.

Under those conditions, when 300 percent of inventory was sold, the 43 percent discount produced a margin of 226 percent of inventory (3 x 75.4). Of that, 173.4 percent was operating cost and 52.6 percent was profit. (Ten percent profit on sales, if average discount is 43 percent and the stock turn is three, equals 52.6 percent profit on inventory.) When the sales level goes up to 375 percent of inventory, the 43 percent discount on the additional 75 percent of sales produces an additional margin of 56.6 percent of the same inventory figure (.75 x .754). Since there is no operating expense to charge against it, the 56.6 percent is profit, slightly more than doubling the previous profit of 52.6 percent on inventory.

These numbers suggest that a returns level of 20 percent (for a store buying at 43 percent discount with a stock turn of three) represents a reduction of approximately 10 percentage points of profit against sales. This applies even to the bookseller who may imagine that making the publisher wait for payment takes some of the curse off poor buying decisions. Even if some of the store's inventory investment is publisher money, the total amount of money available for book stock (including past-due accounts payable) is limited, if only by the size of the debt the publisher will permit. That total amount — the store's own money, the money borrowed from banks, the money owed to publishers — is what the bookseller has available for investment in inventory. As we have said, and will say again, investing that money wisely is probably the single most important element in the successful operation of a bookstore.

Returns are undoubtedly the consequence of faulty buying decisions. It may be that a title was mistakenly chosen. Almost invariably, the title was right but the quantity was wrong — too many copies were bought. The bookseller did not intend to make a bad decision. Sometimes it was the temptation of the publisher's special discount offer, or dated billing, or some other sales blandishment. Frequently, the bookseller, making the mistake of trying to look months into the future, was overly concerned with the danger of the "lost sale."

Of course, there is a sales rep sitting across the desk, coaxing the bookseller to take more, holding up the "carrot" of better terms — dated billing, higher discounts, co-op advertising — and hinting at the stick of lost sales from under-ordering lead titles. But the bookstore probably loses more sales on titles that were not stocked because inventory money was tied up in too many copies of the titles it did have. When this idea is fully appreciated, the bookseller may invest just as many dollars as before in inventory, but will do so in smaller quantities of more titles. And, while it is too much to expect that such a change will transform imperfect buying that leads to returns into brilliant buying that leads to riches, it will certainly lead to improvement.

The returns problem for bookstore management has been given a new twist in recent years. The bookseller is now frequently presented with the "opportunity" to solve the returns problem and improve margins by buying "nonreturnable." More and more publishers, at their wits' end to solve the high returns "problem" they have themselves created, offer to barter the bookseller the right to return unsold books in exchange for additional (usually about five points) discount. One would imagine, from the simple fact that the deal is being pushed by publishers, that it is to the publishers' advantage to have the bookseller accept.

Although it is beside the point in our discussion of what the bookseller's buying strategy should be, it is our opinion that the offer is not in the publisher's own best interest because, even at higher discounts, it makes the bookseller reluctant to buy. Offering a nonreturnable discount option demonstrates the publishers' failure to appreciate why the right of return was instituted in the first place (by the publishers themselves, unilaterally, of course) back in the 1930s, as well as the degree to which that right has fueled the expansion of bookselling and, therefore, of publishing itself. Most incomprehensible, it indicates a refusal to recognize that publishers, who are the ones who pressure the bookseller to buy more, can reduce returns without changing their terms, simply by selling more realistically.

But that is the publishers' problem.

What should the bookseller's response be to the offer to buy nonreturnable?

Although we have pointed out again and again that discount has much less value than it is usually assigned, it is, nevertheless, of some value. If the five points of additional discount will have no effect on the bookseller's buying decisions — and we must assume that the booksellers who have accepted the offer believe exactly that — it would be as foolish to turn the extra points away as it is foolish of the publisher to offer them. But to what degree is that likely, or even possible?

The right of return was inaugurated by publishers to reduce the apparent potential cost to the bookseller of a positive buying error — either choosing the wrong title or ordering too many copies — in order to relax the bookseller's normally defensive stance toward new, untried titles entering the store. When the danger that the store will be stuck with unsold copies hangs over the buying decision, the bookseller's defensive caution is exaggerated.

When the right to return was introduced, the bookseller's willingness to accept more titles was clearly demonstrated. The opposite effect was demonstrated rather dramatically in 1980, when Harcourt Brace Jovanovich (now Harcourt Brace & Company) withdrew the right of return and granted booksellers *more than ten points of discount* in compensation. Harcourt trade sales almost disappeared — so dramatically that the right to return was promptly restored.

It is true that in what was supposed to be a trail-blazing experiment, Harcourt did not give booksellers a choice of accepting or rejecting the no-returns conditions. The implosion of buying was not, however, due to lack of choice; it was clearly the result of exaggerated bookseller caution due to the realization that an unforeseen error can be truly costly. Since that occasional error could only be from *over*buying rather than *under*buying, booksellers made absolutely certain that overbuying would not occur.

The fact that the bookseller's caution is based on sound, solid reason — the danger of being stuck with unsold books, perhaps even single copies of various titles — does not alter the result, which is that fewer books come into the store to be available for sale to the public. It is no help to tell the bookseller — which the publisher's rep will surely do — that, for many of the titles being offered, the likelihood of unsalable overstock is small. The danger may be small, but the penalty is large. The danger is there, and the bookseller is very much aware of it. The only sure way to avoid it is to buy only the titles that are virtually guaranteed to sell, and to buy even those in modest quantities, reordering only titles showing very strong public response.

We have said that the invention, in the early 1930s, of the right to return was responsible for a dramatic expansion in retail bookselling. It changed bookselling from an amateur hobby for retired teachers on a pension to a legitimate business, attractive to entrepreneurs and graduates of business schools. The bookseller welcomed the right to return, because the nature of books puts the retailer at much greater risk than the retailer of shirts or office furniture. The range of product in any haberdashery or dealer in office furniture is narrow enough to permit the store to choose product with reasonable expertise and to recommend product knowledgeably to the store's customers. The bookseller does not and cannot "know" the wide variety of products in the bookstore in the same way. On top of the inevitable lack of intimate knowledge of the full range of the store's inventory, the bookseller carries a bewilderingly broader inventory, many items in one copy, to be sure. Can you imagine a haberdashery or office furniture dealer offering an assortment of 180,000 "titles," or 100,000, 50,000, or even 5,000?

The bookseller needs the right of return to feel secure in stocking the store with enough merchandise to make the business viable. No discount advantage can be a satisfactory substitute. Bill Jovanovich proved that. A high discount without the right to return transforms bookselling from a business into a "crapshoot." If there is to be gambling in books, it belongs with the publisher, who has the time and interest to read every title — not with the bookseller, who performs an essential service that makes the publisher's business possible.

The shrinkage in sales experienced by Harcourt Brace Jovanovich way back in 1980, and the shrinkages being experienced currently by publishers following a more cautious version of that gambit — which would be evident to them if they analyzed their sales in detail — reduces the movement of publishers' books *into* the stores. It should not be overlooked, however, that reducing the movement of books *into* the stores reduces the movement of books *out* of the stores. The sales loss to the publisher represents a corresponding sales loss *to the bookseller.*

This reduction in sales will not show up in "special orders," books presold before they are bought from the publisher. It certainly will show up on advance orders in more titles skipped and distinctly smaller quantities (all to the good, in itself) on titles that cannot be skipped. More serious, it will shrivel up reordering except for the most obvious and strongest titles.

It is a completely human reaction to a real set of (somewhat exaggerated) dangers. The bookseller who tries to fight that instinct by deliberately buying more freely will join the pack after the inevitable overstocks, however small, show up here and there around the store.

Is it worth accepting a reduced flow of books through the store in exchange for five points of discount? Unless that reduction in the flow of books will truly be very small, probably not. Publishers may eventually discover that the no-returns option shoots publishers in the foot, and withdraw the offer. But even if that does not happen, ask some bookseller friends about their purchases from such publishers before and after the offer to buy nonreturnable was accepted. Or, if you are among those who accepted that offer, examine your own records in detail and be guided accordingly.

A bookseller, buying without the right to return, will stock a narrower assortment of titles. A narrower assortment of titles in the store means lower sales and, as customers realize there is less to choose from and stop dropping in to browse, disproportionately lower sales. And profits will drop faster than sales. Returns can and should be avoided by any number of planned approaches to buying, but the right to return is too critical to trade away.

Discounting: What It Does and What It Costs

The widespread practice of discounting and its apparent minor effect on a store's economic health is another indication of the relative importance of turn and discount. There is not much question that discounting increases sales, but whether it does so enough, and whether the bookseller adapts buying policy to keep stock turn high, is another matter.

Discounting — selling books at some percentage below the publisher's "suggested" retail price — has been a major or minor feature of bookselling as far back as anyone can remember. During the late 1800s, it became so intense — leading to artificially high retail prices and increases in discounts to booksellers — that publishers and booksellers joined together to encourage "net pricing."

Beginning about 1902, the American Booksellers Association and the newly formed American Publishers Association tried to enforce price maintenance on the legal pretext that copyright gave the publisher control over the selling price to the public. Investing great effort, they managed to get near unanimous conformity among publishers and booksellers. By 1912, *Publishers Weekly* was editorializing that "the book trade during the past few years when fixed prices have in general replaced the old undercutting practices, has begun to regain its former prosperity."

Yet, even then, there was one outstanding retail holdout — Macy's department store — which would torpedo the whole scheme. Although some publishers would not sell to them directly, Macy's bought books in roundabout ways and often sold them below cost, reminding the public of that fact through extensive advertising.

Publishers Weekly (and the publishers and booksellers) complained that Macy's was using book price-cutting to buy store traffic. The publishers sued Macy's, and Macy's sued the publishers, and the cases made their way slowly and erratically through the lower courts while Macy's continued discounting. Finally, on December 1, 1913, the U.S. Supreme Court ruled in favor of Macy's and price-cutting became a standard fixture of department-store book sections. In the 1930s, as Macy's and Gimbel's book departments tried to outdo one another, I remember going downtown to buy Modern Library books for 19¢ and 20¢ each.

Though ghosts of department-store book sections still exist, their power as book retailers or discounters is a thing of the past.

Today, we have a new wave of book discounting, inspired primarily by the intense retailing competition introduced by the bookstore chains. The aim of discounting is no longer to help department stores sell furniture or ladies dresses; it is to help bookstores sell more books. Or, sometimes, in its present incarnation, discounting is intended to make it very rough on the bookseller down the street who cannot afford to do it.

The exceptional, prominent identification of the "retail price" right on the product makes discounting a much more dramatic competitive device in the retailing of books than it is for other merchandise.

There are three valid reasons for discounting from the

retail price. The first and most obvious is to gain a customer — to entice someone into the store, attracted by the discount, who will, at least once in a while, also purchase something else. The second reason is to forestall losing a customer — someone who would otherwise be attracted to a competitor's store by the discounted titles available there. The third, and least obvious, reason is to trade a lower return on sales for a higher return on investment.

If the bookseller buys an item on January 2 for 55¢ (a discount of 45 percent) and sells it for $1 on December 31, the 55¢ investment has earned an annual return of 45¢. If an identical item is bought on January 2 for 55¢ and sold at a 20 percent discount for 80¢ on April 1, the 55¢ investment has earned a return of 25¢. If 55¢ from that sale is used to purchase another copy, which is sold on August 2 for 80¢, that 55¢ investment has earned 50¢; and if the retailer does it a third time, the 55¢ investment will have earned, in that year, 75¢ on items discounted 20 percent, compared with the 45¢ earned on the item sold in one year at full retail with no discount to the consumer.

A clodhopper of a footnote must be added. The 25¢ return on the 55¢ investment per copy applies if only one copy is bought by the bookseller — unlikely if it is a title being discounted. If ten copies are bought, each 80¢ sale results in a 25¢ return against an investment of $5.50; if one hundred copies are bought, each sale returns 25¢ against a $55 investment. Depending on the relation of rate of sale to quantity purchased, it is possible that, even with an impressive rate of sale, the discounted title could earn substantially less against investment than a title sold at full retail.

Or, discounting can be seen from a more strategic viewpoint.

Suppose a bookseller is buying at 45 percent discount and currently earns a profit of 5 percent on sales. If retail prices are cut by 20 percent across the board, the margin on sales for the bookseller shrinks from 45 percent to 25 percent. Prior to discounting, if profit was 5 percent (out of the 45 percent discount/margin), the expenses of operating the store represented 40 percent of sales.

We can assume that the operating cost does not change substantially even if discounting creates a surge of business. The clerks and cash registers will be cheerfully busier but able to handle the added burden.

Discounting reduces the percentage of the retail price available to cover operating costs and profit. At 20 percent off retail, the bookseller would aim to cover both the operating expense (40 percent of previous sales volume) and (at least) the 5 percent profit from the new margin of 25 percent, reduced from the previous 45 percent. The increase in sales required to do this is the old margin of 45 percent divided by the new margin of 25 percent, which is 1.8. The magic number in our hypothetical case is therefore 80 percent. An increase in sales of 80 percent of books discounted by 20 percent will produce as much margin as the lower level of sales did at full retail price. Sales above the critical 80 percent increase would contribute a handsome 25 percent of sales to the total profit of the store.

That short-cut calculation is easy to check. The margin at 45 percent discount before discounting to the public is the .45 discount divided by the .55 cost, or 82¢ per dollar of sales. At an effective 25 percent discount from retail (after discounting to the consumer), the margin, the .25 discount divided by the .55 cost, drops to 45.5¢, which, multiplied by 1.8, would restore the old margin of 82¢. If the increase in sales is less than 80 percent, discounting will have been costly to the bookseller. At a 70 percent increase, in our example, expenses would be covered but the store's profit would be cut in half, to 2.5 percent. If the increase in sales were only 60 percent, profit would be wiped out completely.

Booksellers buying from vendors at different discounts and/or offering different discounting incentives to their customers would be working against correspondingly different "magic numbers" and toward correspondingly different rewards. This arithmetic does not consider stock turn. It is clearly possible to achieve the targeted increases in sales on the discounted titles from large inventory stocks — it will certainly seem easier. A satisfactory return on investment, however, requires even more attention to frequent purchasing in small quantities on discounted titles to prevent a high return on sales (generated by a sales increase higher than 80 percent in our example) from masking a sharp decline in return on investment. Careful attention to stock turn is unavoidable.

To profit from discounting, the bookseller must not only increase the sale sufficiently and get the increase speedily; the bookseller must also hold inventory down and replenish stock frequently.

Conclusion

We have tried to demonstrate that there is much more valid, objective, mathematical guidance possible than the simple comparison of discount rates on the bookseller's orders, particularly as these discount comparisons frequently point to the wrong decisions. It is safe to assume that, whatever decision is required — from simple book buying to the more complicated questions of discounting, allocating floor space, transferring to a new location, or opening a branch store — many of the factors can be quantified and a simple arithmetical manipulation can offer more reliable guidance than subjective expert judgment. Being humble enough to hold your own expertise in abeyance and taking the trouble to look for mathematical relationships will usually be well worth the trouble.

About the Author

Leonard Shatzkin is the author of *"In Cold Type"* (Houghton Mifflin, 1982), a critical discussion of book publishing and distribution in the United States. He has held executive positions for over thirty-five years in a number of publishing houses, covering wide areas of responsibility, including retail bookselling, production, editorial, marketing and sales, and warehousing and shipping. He was production manager at The Viking Press and at Doubleday Book Company as well as vice-president at both McGraw-Hill and Crowell-Collier Macmillan. When Crowell-Collier bought the Brentano bookstore chain, it was placed under Shatzkin's direction.

While at Doubleday, Shatzkin hired George Blagowidow to develop a mathematical method to predict advance sale so printing decisions could be made earlier and more accurately. In the first year of operation, this prediction system resulted in direct savings of a quarter million dollars and, for the first time in memory, not a single Doubleday title was sold as overstock and no title was out of stock for even one day.

The sales prediction method later provided the means for measuring the effectiveness of the sales force, nationally and by region. Shatzkin was put in charge of applying these guides to improve sales force productivity. In the five years from the resulting expansion of the sales force until Shatzkin left Doubleday, sales increased almost fourfold, with no discernible change in number or mix of published titles.

An offshoot of the sales prediction system, later adapted for inventory control at the bookstore level, generated the Doubleday Merchandising Plan, under which the titles and quantities of Doubleday titles were mathematically controlled in the retail stores that enrolled in the plan. The sale of Doubleday titles doubled in participating stores; the profitability of Doubleday books for Gimbel's, because of better stock turn, higher discounts, and reduced returns, increased thirteen times! At its height, the Doubleday Merchandising Plan was operating in 800 stores.

In 1978, Shatzkin became an independent consultant in book retailing, publishing, and manufacturing. His clients have included Doubleday, the Ford Foundation, CBS International Publishing, Dodd Mead, Grolier, St. Martin's Press, General Mills, Avon Products, Macmillan, and John Wiley.

He has written extensively on the book industry in *Publishers Weekly, American Bookseller, Daedalus, Book Production Industries, Library Quarterly,* and other journals, and has lectured to publishers groups in Sweden, Denmark, Norway, Spain, Mexico, Yugoslavia, Cuba, and other countries.

Printed in the United States
76972LV00006B/254

9 780878 380